MW01101003

BUILDING a
LEGENDARY
LEADER

BUILDING a LEGENDARY LEADER:

The Architecture of Crafting Managerial-Leadership Greatness, One Week at a Time!

Business/Leadership/Management/Self Help

Library of Congress
Cataloging-in-Publication Data

Magee, Jeffrey L. Ph.D., P.D.M., C.S.P., C.M.C.
BUILDING a LEGENDARY LEADER: The Architecture of Crafting
Managerial-Leadership Greatness, One Week at a Time!

Grant, Kathryn, second editor
Hannesson, Robb, project manager
Jones, Joy, first editor
Jurgensen, Tim, book cover design
Shoemaker, John, photographer

No portion of this book can be used in any manner without the written
permission of the author or publisher.

© 2003 by Jeffrey L. Magee, Ph.D., P.D.M., C.S.P., C.M.C.

For information regarding special discounts for bulk purchases for
business training emersion, large groups, families and gifts, please
contact the following:

PERFORMANCE Publishing
P.O. Box 701918
Tulsa, OK 74170-1918
Toll free 1-877-90-MAGEE or
918-499-8870

www.JeffreyMagee.com

ISBN: 0-9718010-0-2

BUILDING a
LEGENDARY
LEADER:
The Architecture of Crafting Managerial-Leadership Greatness, One Week at a Time!

By: Jeffrey Magee, Ph.D., P.D.M., C.S.P., C.M.C.

BUILDING a LEGENDARY LEADER!
ISBN: 0-9718010-0-2
U.S. $29.95
Copyright 2003

Table of Contents

Foreword   Page 15
                        Legendary Leaders Among Us
Introduction   Page 17
                        Building a Legendary Leader

SECTION ONE: *Mentoring*
Chapter 1   Page 23
                        Mentoring Future Leaders: Setting
                        the Framework for Success
Chapter 2   Page 27
                        Mentoring Future Leaders: Five Step
                        Mentor Process
Chapter 3   Page 31
                        Mentoring Future Leaders: Five Step
                        Communication Accountability
                        Formula
Chapter 4   Page 35
                        Mentoring Future Leaders: The Well
                        Within

SECTION TWO: *Thought Leaders*
Chapter 5   Page 41
                        Developing Thought Leader
                        Capacity: Organizational Objectivity
Chapter 6   Page 45
                        Developing Thought Leader
                        Capacity: Trait Characteristics
Chapter 7   Page 49
                        Developing Thought Leader
                        Capacity: Experience Driven

Chapter 8   Page 53
                           Developing Thought Leader
                           Capacity: Model of Replication

SECTION THREE: *Motivating*
Chapter 9   Page 59
                           Motivating the Individual Within
Chapter 10   Page 63
                           Motivating the Team You Connect
                           With
Chapter 11   Page 67
                           Motivating Oneself
Chapter 12   Page 73
                           Motivating Relationships Together

SECTION FOUR: *Building Political Capital*
Chapter 13   Page 79
                           Building Political Capital: One
                           Partnership "Decision" at a Time
Chapter 14   Page 83
                           Building Political Capital: Selecting
                           Fast Partners Via "Rule 80-10-10"
Chapter 15   Page 87
                           Building Political Capital:
                           "Deposits" and "Withdraws" to
                           Relationships
Chapter 16   Page 91
                           Building Political Capital: Saving
                           Face and Bouncing Back From
                           Controversy

SECTION FIVE: *Independent Thought*
Chapter 17   Page 97
                           Independent Thought: Self-
                           Accountability With Integrity

Chapter 18   Page 101
                     Independent Thought: Sustaining a
                     Lonely Position
Chapter 19   Page 105
                     Independent Thought: Weathering
                     the Storm Of Criticism

SECTION SIX: ***Centering***
Chapter 20   Page 111
                     Centering Yourself and Staying
                     Grounded
Chapter 21   Page 115
                     Centering Others For Their
                     Greatness Within
Chapter 22   Page 119
                     Centering the Workplace
                     Environment for Success: The Most
                     Overlooked Ingredient

SECTION SEVEN: ***Conflict Management***
Chapter 23   Page 127
                     Conflict Management MAPs to
                     Success
Chapter 24   Page 131
                     Conflict Management 4-Engagement
                     Options, The L-grid
Chapter 25   Page 135
                     Conflict Management, The Anatomy
                     Intervention Model

SECTION EIGHT: ***Life Balance***
Chapter 26   Page 141
                     Life Balance as a Leader: From 97
                     Percent to 3 Percent

Chapter 27	Page 147
	Life Balance as a Leader: Life-Cycle Direction
Chapter 28	Page 151
	Life Balance as a Leader: Time to Leave

SECTION NINE: ***Leadership Engagement***

Chapter 29	Page 157
	Leadership Engagement: Six Intervention Styles
Chapter 30	Page 163
	Leadership Engagement: Instant Identification and Succession Planning Made Easy
Chapter 31	Page 169
	Leadership Engagement: "Span-Of-Control" Drives Empowerment
Chapter 32	Page 173
	Leadership Engagement: The 5W's and 1H of Intervention

SECTION TEN: ***Generational Connectedness***

Chapter 33	Page 179
	Generational Connectedness: The Next Leadership Paradigm Shift to the Five Segmentations in Your Business
Chapter 34	Page 183
	Generational Connectedness: Unique Traits and Motivators of the Five Segmentations Within and Outside of Your Business

Chapter 35   Page 187
                      Generational Connectedness: Future
                      Challenges and Opportunities for
                      Blending the Five Segmentations
                      You Lead

SECTION ELEVEN: Controlled Risk Taking
Chapter 36   Page 193
                      Controlled Risk Taking and Decision
                      Making: Facilitating the Decision
                      Process Via The STOP Model
Chapter 37   Page 197
                      Controlled Risk Taking and Decision
                      Making: Gaining Consensus and
                      Buy-In Via The SMART Model
Chapter 38   Page 201
                      Controlled Risk Taking and Decision
                      Making: Engaging the Four Core
                      Stakeholders as Allies
Chapter 39   Page 205
                      Controlled Risk Taking and Decision
                      Making: Finding Optimal Quality
                      and Determining When to Take
                      Action

SECTION TWELVE: Leadership Ethics
Chapter 40   Page 211
                      Leadership Ethics: Seven Ethical
                      Rules for Guiding Leadership
                      Behavior
Chapter 41   Page 215
                      Leadership Ethics: One's Character
                      for Rent or Forecasted
Chapter 42   Page 219
                      Leadership Ethics: Modeling It Daily

Chapter 43   Page 223
                    Leadership Ethics: Legacy Factor

SECTION THIRTEEN: *Loyalty Advantage*
Chapter 44   Page 231
                    Loyalty Advantage: Becoming Other
                    Person Centered
Chapter 45   Page 235
                    Loyalty   Advantage: Increasing
                    Loyalty With Others
Chapter 46   Page 239
                    Loyalty Advantage: Moving Beyond
                    Blame

SECTION FOURTEEN: *Entitlement Mentality*
Chapter 47   Page 245
                    Entitlement Mentality: The Creation
                    of One's Own Problem Child
Chapter 48   Page 251
                    Entitlement Mentality: Eroding a
                    Team, One Me'ism at a Time
Chapter 49   Page 257
                    Entitlement Mentality: Working for
                    FAIR not EQUAL Playing Status

SECTION FIFTEEN: *Assessment Instruments*
Chapter 50   Page 263
                    Assessment to Success:
                    Interviewing for Impact and Building
                    Winning Teams
Chapter 51   Page 269
                    Assessment to Success: What Gets
                    Measured, Gets Measured!

SECTION SIXTEEN: Conclusion
Chapter 52   Page 277
                   Building A Legendary Leader: The
                   Evolving and Continuing Process

ABOUT THE AUTHOR
Author Bio   Page 281
                   Author Background, Web site
                   Address, Reader Opportunities and
                   Offers

REINFORCEMENT TOOLS
Pocket Card   Page 283
                   Wallet Reminder Card

Foreword

A legendary leader does not wait for tomorrow, they do it now!

Changing the world we live in, by building tomorrow's leaders today, has been the fundamental purpose of the United States Junior Chamber/USJaycees for decades. The legendary leaders among us can be seen in many places. Business leaders, civic leaders, association leaders, and world leaders can be traced back to their roots within the USJaycees organization.

Whether your path takes you through small town America, across major urban sprawl or to the communities and small towns across the international terrain, you can find leaders engaged in the Junior Chamber International, the largest leadership development organization on the planet.

Serving as a universe through which individuals can learn, grow and experience the challenges and victories of developing others to greatness, leaders build a legacy with their every act – whether good or bad!

A legendary leader can be born and created. Leaders possess unique traits and abilities and they are willing to tap into them for the benefit of others. A legendary leader has within them a never-ending desire to make both the place they occupy and the people within it better than they were when they arrived.

This book, *BUILDING A LEGENDARY LEADER* provides the architecture for building a legacy worth being proud of. It provides the architecture for organizations to create conducive environments for leaders to develop and succeed!

The legendary leader recognizes that their true legacy will not be measured by what they do today, but from that which grows out of it in the years to come.

Anyone can talk a legacy, only a true leader does it now!

Mike Faller, 83rd President
United States Junior Chamber
www.USJAYCEES.org

Introduction

BUILDING A LEGENDARY LEADER: The Architecture of Crafting Managerial-Leadership Greatness, One Week at a Time! The floodgate of leadership books available today by academies and individuals who have never led a successful group or held a meaningful position of leadership within an organization is amazing . . . and yet, more books keep arriving daily to the marketplace.

I have long wondered what would happen if you took most of the popular names in business-management writing and asked for their real world work resumes, the number of paychecks they have ever signed, or the degree of functional positions they have actually held. How many of them would need more than a Post-It Note?

With this book, the leader within you will be fed the nutrients it has longed for in order to grow to the next level of leadership effectiveness. You will become truly inspired to greatness. And, those around you will become inspired to greatness as well.

In studying leadership greatness, this book will afford you a unique vantage point.

From the perspective of a Certified Management Consultant (CMC), research and actual hands-on work with the Fortune 100, interacting and designing leadership development training initiatives with the two largest leadership organizations on the planet — the United States ARMY and the United States Junior Chamber (USJaycees), writing about it weekly in my syndicated leadership columns, appearing on stage internationally as a Certified Speaking Professional (CSP) before tens-of-thousands annually, and practicing it with my own staff daily ... (Paragraph doesn't make much sense)

> *I have learned that if it does not work,*
> *It does not work, and that*
> *I will be held accountable daily and instantly!*

BUILDING A LEGENDARY LEADER: The Architecture Of Crafting Managerial-Leadership Greatness, One Week At A Time, takes a refreshing look at core leadership traits from the perspective of competency-based skills. As you evolve as an inspired leader, certain talent pools you posses will be richer than others.

The degree of greatness from merely being another leader and becoming a legendary leader may be very slight ... and the slight variance you build upon will distinguish you within your business and from those around you.

Each week from my syndicated leadership columns that appear nationally in business newspapers, an electronic subscription version is crafted and sent to our clients and subscribers. These *"eLeadership Moments"* are always content-rich and deliver to individuals' managerial and leadership skill development techniques on a weekly basis. Skill technique, if used and adapted by individuals, will further develop their leadership skill set and sustain greater levels of growth and success.

You can subscribe to a weekly dose of *LEADERSHIP DEVELOPMENT skill based ideas* in the form of an eArticle at www.JeffreyMagee.com.

Becoming an inspired leader – one to whom others look toward, seek counsel from and gage their actions – is a mark of a true LEGENDARY LEADER!

Within business today, it is, in fact, the business of everyone to continually develop business and inspire leadership at all levels. Business leaders of the past two decades have been through the cascade of downsizing, right sizing and reengineering to survive. Now the focus must evolve towards both the operational growth and operational excellence of the system side of the business and the personnel assets for the future.

This book details the unique traits and abilities demonstrated daily by legendary leaders across industry, across geography, and across cultural and individual barriers. Learn the fifteen power ingredients to becoming a LEGENDARY LEADER!

A LEGENDARY LEADER'S legacy is that which can be measured after they are gone from the presence of others and the organization of which they have stewardship!

SECTION ONE:
Mentoring

Chapter 1	Mentoring Future Leaders: Setting the Framework for Success
Chapter 2	Mentoring Future Leaders: Five-Step Mentor Process
Chapter 3	Mentoring Future Leaders: Five-Step Communication Accountability Formula
Chapter 4	Mentoring Future Leaders: Tapping The Well Within

Chapter ONE
Mentoring Future Leaders: Setting the Framework for Success Within an Organization

"The best executive is the one who has sense enough to pick good men (women), to do what he (she) wants done, and the self restraint to keep from meddling with them while they do it."
- Theodore Roosevelt, 26th president of the United States

Where have all the leaders gone? Where can you find a real leader today? The state of leadership within organizations today is at a critical point, and how senior leaders decide to act now will dictate what we experience tomorrow!

To listen to and observe senior leadership today, whether within the military (alarmingly, far too many senior officers are no longer cognizant of basic functional operations they are given, nor capable of running around the block without a needed trip to the hospital), within government (managers appear incapable of getting employees to work together, and accept a dysfunctional environment – you can barely get rid of a bad employee without an act of Congress) or within the business place (whereby the protectionist mindset, to keep one's own job, of mid-level managers causes a guarded interaction with others), would lead an outside observer to conclude that leadership development is evaporating before our vary eyes.

Far too often, it seems great followers and future leaders are stymied by poor and ineffective organizational leadership development programs and opportunities. Recent studies by the American Business Institute, which have been reinforced by a client survey by JMI, revealed some powerful reasons that this mindset may be breeding.

Shockingly, survey data consistently revealed that the first mindset of a man, when promoted in the workplace, is around the theme of, "What must I do to get the next promotion, and how fast?" Whereby the first mindset of a woman promoted in the workplace centers around, "What is expected of me in this new position in order to succeed?"

A simple solution is to establish an environmental mindset of growing successful future leaders. Also, place present leaders on notice through active participation in some sort of a **"Leadership Mentor Development Program."** Some guideposts for designing an effective mentoring approach to cultivating and growing true leaders are:

?   Select solid performers (not political lackies) that are at least two direct report positions from the individual to be mentored. This positional space between the mentor and mentee allows for greater interaction and giving on the part of the mentor.

?   Allow the relationship to be both 'Formal' (measurement protocols and assignments) and 'Informal" (conversational and relationship driven) in contact.

?   Have predetermined objectives for both the mentor and mentee. An objective is a means by which to measure and hold all parties accountable. Most organizations, in their efforts to remain competitive in the past, have actually created their vary problems of the present, by expecting great leaders from within to step forward and lead teams to greatness. By creating competitive environments within, individuals choose to partake in the activities that get rewarded. For most, this seems to be a question of, "How do I attract the spotlight directly to me in a favorable manner and do so at any cost?"

? The costs of the past will pay heavy penalties in our future unless senior leaders remove reality blinders and institute rigorous developmental programs to ensure a prosperous future.

Chapter TWO
Mentoring Future Leaders: A Five-Step Formal Mentor System for Your Organization

"When the student is ready, the teacher will reveal himself."
- *Unknown, as told by Mentor,*
Jim Stovall, CEO, Narrative Television Network

Where have all the leaders gone? How do you cultivate a leader within? In today's demanding work environment, everyone must have a little leader within themselves, and at times, a real leader is needed to step forward and lead others to greatness.

To do so takes an active and systematic approach to developing those within an organization. A model for an effective **"Leadership Mentor Development Program"** may incorporate a five-step approach. Consider candidate participation at these levels:

1. **Mentor Level One** – an **elementary mentor**, whereby the mentor possesses great basic knowledge and patience of a subject matter, which needs to be instilled into another person.

2. **Mentor Level Two** – the graduation of the mentor to a **secondary mentor**, who can provide opportunities to the mentee to apply this new basic knowledge or skill. This secondary mentor serves as a contact person for the mentee while they are being

drilled in the application of this knowledge, and assists them in becoming both comfortable and proficient with this knowledge base. This person may serve as a go-to contact for the mentee, when they can't connect with or don't feel comfortable connecting with their boss.

3. **Mentor Level Three** – a **post secondary mentor**, who has the capacity to constructively challenge the mentee to seek new applications for this knowledge base and encourage them to seek greatness with it. This mentor must recognize the ways in which the mentee has effectively applied this knowledge and the talents that the mentee has further developed in varying places within an organization – cross-functional applications are directed by this mentor to the mentee.

4. **Mentor Level Four** – a **master mentor**, who has a well-positioned network of stakeholders and decision-makers across both the internal organization and external world. Without the mentee knowing it, they can serve to promote the mentee to others.

5. **Mentor Level Five** – the level that a mentee has attained by growth and development from level one to level four. The mentee has demonstrated a grasp and application of knowledge and experience, and has therefore earned the right to become a mentor as well. Now the process reverses with a **reverse mentor** relationship ability.

This model may serve as a powerful template to dictate, very specifically, what the responsibilities may be for each level in the mentor-to-mentee development life cycle.

At this point, another critical question arises. Now that there is an objective means of measuring the developmental progress of a mentee, who is qualified to serve as a mentor? First-level considerations in selecting, recruiting or accepting nominations/applications for mentors are:

1. A willingness on the part of the mentor to invest his or her time and energy into the mentee is critical for this growth relationship to develop present and future leaders for organizations today.

2. A reservoir of knowledge by the mentor, in terms of both formal and informal knowledge, training and skill certification, that can be deposited into a willing mentee, and thus, enable a shorter learning curve to develop.

3. An accomplished and dedicated senior member, who may be of the present mindset that, because of their tenure, they are no longer valued and appreciated, can be an ideal candidate. This participation opportunity may be just the prescription for a renewed energy.

4. A person with a genuine vested interest in the organization's success and core survival will be an exceedingly diligent mentor, who takes the mentee's interests to heart.

A fast track to **"Leadership Mentor Development Program"** failure is expecting or accepting into participation an individual who does not adhere to any of the above benchmark suggestions.

An Ohio State University study indicated that professional women in the work place with mentor relationships, versus those with no mentor relationships, were up to 68 times more likely to be promoted and marketed in their careers. The question for organizations and managerial-leaders to ask now is, "Can we afford not to invest in our personnel's assets by not having a mentor program?"

"If a man empties his pyres into his head, no one can take it away from him. An investment in knowledge always pays the best interest."
- Benjamin Franklin, Inventor, Statesman, Writer

Chapter THREE
Mentoring Future Leaders: Five-Step Communication Accountability Formula

"There is a story in Arabic which tells of a pupil asking a wise man how he could become a good conversationalist. The sage replied, 'Listen, my son.' After waiting a while, the pupil said, 'I am listening. Please continue your instruction.' The sage smiled. 'There is no more to tell.'"
- As told by Ali Karakus, Turkish Exchange Student in America

Communication connection between mentor and mentee is critical for a relationship to develop and a mentee to grow into a powerful leader.

Far too often, a communication exchange leaves two people with two different understandings of what was said and what is to be done. It is these miscommunications that can lead to a breakdown in communication connections.

To ensure an effective systematic communication connection in business, consider this simple five-step model, used in everything from executive coaching to therapy sessions between doctors and clients. A mentor and mentee must communicate one step at a time, ensuring buy-in at each level before progressing onward to the next step.

1. Establish a will to **buy-in, or even enroll into, a conversation** on the subject matter you are putting forth. If the other party is unwilling to acknowledge

and buy into that subject matter, there will be no communication connection. In essence, seek permission to connect, and ensure the other party is willing to connect before expecting to proceed.

2. Make a connection to the subject matter being raised to the other person's **vested interest level**. In essence, make the connection to what they say they are all about ... their *identity* and *purpose* should be connected to the subject.

3. Jointly discuss the varied **choices** that the mentee is willing to make to ensure that what they are enrolling into actually materializes.

4. From the range of choices that can be made to execute the enrolled issue, and for a successful communication connection to materialize, there must be at least two action items that the mentee will **commit** to.

5. In order for any communication connection to actually take place, both parties need to clearly discuss and agree, precisely, how to hold all parties **accountable** to this connection plan of five steps. In essence, how will you objectively know if you are on track, off track, ahead of schedule, or behind schedule?

Investing valuable time into the growth and development of another person can be quickly sabotaged if the parties cannot connect communicatively. Studies reveal that one of the leading contributors to dysfunctional organization rests at the door of ineffective communication among individuals.

"Wise men talk because they have something to say; fools because they would like to say something."
Plato

Chapter FOUR
Mentoring Future Leaders: Tapping the Well Within

"Strong lives are motivated by dynamic purposes; lesser ones exist on wishes and inclinations. The most glowing successes are but reflections of an inner fire."
- Kenneth Hildebrand, American Clergyman

As a leader within an organization, and in an attempt to grow and mentor future leaders, ask yourself these critical questions:

1. How deep is your well?
2. How many wells do you possess within yourself?
3. Are you dipping into the wrong well?
4. Have you gone to the well one too many times?

The magic and poetry of great management and leadership today is when one has that rare encounter with a person, who seems to overflow with the greatness of giving that which they have mastered.

Have you ever noticed that within an individual are wells of greatness? These wells are filled with the specific knowledge, talents, experiences, self-beliefs and abilities that one possesses. These are the wells to which one goes when applying energies toward accomplishing an activity or endeavor.

To excel as a true managerial-leader and inspire those on your team to greatness, start by demonstrating a passion for living from your inner wells, which run the deepest and greatest. Identify those wells within you, which truly flow freely and create a high level of energy and excitement. It is from these wells that one should live. It is from these wells that a true managerial-leader realizes he/she should serve to draw from when engaging others.

The same model can guide today's manager or leader in designing effective workflow for employees. Ask yourself, "Do I know which wells run the deepest within our employees? Are appropriate assignments tasked to them?"

Another critical question for organizations to ask and analyze is which wells of proficiency individuals must possess in order to be effective participants in an organization's success. These are the wells of experience, knowledge, training, positions, and so on, which must be cultivated, matured, and rewarded!

A great case for building a **"Leadership Mentor Development Program"** comes from countless surveys and studies with organizations and individuals engaged in such pursuits. Results from a survey of over 300 organizations (by 'Retention and Staffing Report,' Manchester Inc.) revealed:

1. 73 percent of respondents saw a direct correlation to retaining good employees from involvement in aggressive mentoring program opportunities.

2. 62 percent felt a direct enhancement to their immediate career development and long term net worth.

3. 66 percent saw a direct connection to their ability to tap in to future leaders.

4. 49 percent felt it placed high-potential performers into a fast track within their career.

Many Fortune 500 clients of ours (JEFF MAGEE INTERNATIONAL/JMI, Inc.) can trace their market dominance and sustained success to, among other factors, their people development from mentored partnerships. We have seen, first hand, the explosive development this concept has provided to companies such as Defense Finance Accounting Services and Pfizer Pharmaceuticals. And we have conversely seen implosion within organizations that have embraced the great idea of people development via mentoring, but not supported or held accountable their team.

For both your personal and professional development, as well as the development of those around you, the reoccurring question becomes: which of your wells should you dip into? And, are those the wells that I should actually being dipping into or are there better wells within me that will provide lasting nourishment?

SECTION TWO:
Thought Leaders

Chapter 5   Developing Thought Leader
                 Capacity: Organizational
                 Objectivity

Chapter 6   Developing Thought Leader
                 Capacity: Trait Characteristics

Chapter 7   Developing Thought Leader
                 Capacity: Experience Driven

Chapter 8   Developing Thought Leader
                 Capacity: Model of Replication

Chapter FIVE
Developing Thought Leader Capacity: Organizational Objectivity in the Face Adversity

"It is incumbent upon a leader to create an atmosphere
conducive for positive participation among its occupants,
as the first and last objective every day.
Only with the atmosphere that invites participation and
success will people live up to the expectations!"
- Jeffrey Magee, Author/Professional Speaker

As a leader within an organization your capacity to think objectively, thoroughly, and creatively on the run is critical to lasting effectiveness.

An organization's ability to cultivate such 'thought leaders' is an essential differentiator between an organization invested in the personnel asset and an organization invested in the superficial asset management.

There are reasons why organizations like General Electric became institutional names for decades. There are also reasons why others never attain such a revered standing. Among the many reasons for this notoriety is their emphasis on personnel asset development and the cultivation of 'thought leaders' among their ascending managerial-leadership ranks!

Becoming a 'Thought Leader' requires:

1. An environment that champions such behavior.

2. Leadership at all levels that condones the constructive challenge of issues, logic, and decisions, without taking it personally.

3. Individuals with a hunger to learn and grow mentally daily.

4. Individuals with a capacity to accept accountability of actions and expectations and not become excuse-seekers.

5. An organization that inspires a self-starter attitude and allows learning to take place in the face of mistakes.

6. And most importantly, an organization that has the capacity to avoid micro-managing aspiring 'thought leaders'.

The inability of organizations to develop or sustain forward movement starts with individuals, departments, and managers, who hesitate with independent thought processes and retreat into a comfort zone of operational conduct, waiting for someone else to make the critical decisions. This hesitancy breeds contempt from within and without for both the individuals of an organization and the organization itself.

This inefficiency adds up to significant cost loss – loss in business growth, loss in customer retention, loss in getting and securing new customers, loss of retaining potential future 'thought leaders,' who ultimately leave for better opportunities, and so on.

To cultivate objective 'thought leaders' for organization success, an atmosphere first must be cultivated and fostered by the organization's core stakeholders, owners, and senior- most leaders. This is the only way the energy can be cultivated throughout the organization.

Chapter SIX
Developing Thought Leader Capacity: Trait Characteristics

"The learning and knowledge that we have is, at the most, but little compared with that of which we are ignorant."
- Plato, Philosopher

As a leader within an organization, your capacity to craft environments for the development of managerial-leaders into 'thought leaders' is critical to sustained success.

An objective model, which can be used to gage ways to cultivate an individual's ability to become a 'thought leader' and what growth emphasis management may need to focus upon, may require several considerations.

Ones ability to engage in critical 'thought processes' can be equated into a formula, in which the letter "R" represents net "Results."

An individual's ability to perform objective and critical 'thought' processes can be represented by the letter "A," which stands for one's net "Abilities."

As a managerial-leader, attempting to cultivate others' abilities to demonstrate 'thought ability' and, subsequently, rise to the level of potential future organizational 'thought leaders,' the following formula – the **"Player Capability Index"** – allows for self evaluation or employee observation (as used in interviews, promotion considerations, assignment tasking, etc.).

To effectively determine the "Ability" or "Capability" from which one will drive their 'thought ability,' start by evaluating the depth of a person's "Training" (letter "T" in the formula). The "T" can be evaluated in two ways, so visualize a square sign associated with the letter "T" or, in essence, "T2." First, thoroughly review all past training one has received. This includes education, training, seminars, certifications, and so on. Any lack of adequate "T," necessary for an individual to be an effective 'thought leader,' would dictate additional or future "T" exposure that would be appropriate.

This "T" would then be complimented by the "Attitude" ("A") one possesses. This "A" can be conditioned further by both professional and personal environments – in other words, an organization's senior-most leadership, as well as its direct supervisors. One's "A" influences how and when a person will draw upon his or her "T" and apply it!

The "T" and the "A" are then complimented by one's "Performance" ("P") in the formula. How one performs activities will directly influence how one sees and perceives things. This also impacts one's ability to objectively and thoroughly perform as a 'thought leader.'

All of these core ingredients (T+A+P), which drive how an individual will see who one is, will be tempered or weighted by one's "Expectations" ("E") in this personal development asset formula. There are two sets of "E's" (so visualize a square sign associated with the letter "E" or, in essence, "E2") that must be considered in determining someone's ability – or potential – to perform as an effective 'thought leader.' One "E" will represent how the candidate's "E" influences how they see themselves and their specific "T+A+P," which they can tap into. The second "E" will be the other party to an engagement – in essence, the "Expectations" of the organization, client or boss.

So the formula would look something like the following:

$$C = \frac{(T2+A+P)}{E2} = R$$

Cultivating 'thought leadership' ability does not just happen – it must be designed. This formula serves as a guidepost for you to reference specific sets of organizational positions, assignments, travel, committees, teams, client interactions, and internal and external exposures, which all drive core experiences. This, in turn, will drive the uniqueness that we see present in effective 'thought leaders' across industry and culture today!

In a 15-year study, Ohio State University and the U.S. Department of Labor tracked the careers of two groups of more than 3,000 workers, who started jobs during two different decades. Contrary to conventional wisdom, the study showed that those individuals who engaged in on-going training and learning initiatives earned over 25 percent more than their peers.

So what does your **"Player Capability Index"** reveal to those you mentor and desire to cultivate to greatness?

Chapter SEVEN
Developing Thought Leader Capacity: Experience Driven

"A great many people think they are thinking when they are really rearranging their prejudices and superstitions."
- Edward R. Murrow, Author, Journalist

Why do some leaders have the capacity for independent thought and others seem incapable of determining when to go to the bathroom without a committee approval or an approving nod from the boss?

In many cases it is the lack of experience in engaging in independent 'thought capacity' that leads to one's own holdback.

The dean of management, Peter Drucker, my repeated personal observations of our Fortune 100 and governmental agency clients and nearly every HR survey of the past 50 years all reveal that the consistent number one derailment to managerial-leadership success is 'people skill' issues. This is even more so than a functional operational issue.

When organizations look to develop their existing bench of future 'thought leaders,' a good place to start the developmental process is to determine, from existing models of effectiveness within one's talent pool, what specific 'experiences' have aided in the sound development of 'thought leader capacity.' Then work to replicate those specific experiences, in order to mold future 'thought leaders!'

Some of the shaping ground experiences that can aid in the development of a well-rounded 'thought leader' should be individual involvement in:

1. **Player involvement as merely a member** of committees, departments, or teams whose net outcomes are substantive to the core purpose of an organization and the functionality of the team deals with both strategic and tactical application issues.

2. **Player involvement as the leader** of committees, departments, or teams whose net outcomes are substantive to the core purpose of an organization and the functionality of the team deals with both strategic and tactical application issues.

3. **Participation with individuals of cross-cultural lines within** an organization.

4. **Participation with individuals of cross-cultural ethnic lines external** to an organization.

5. **Participation with senior leaders** of your organization in multiple hands-on activities that have medium and long-term engagement exposures.

6. **Final accountability for activities or projects that truly matter** to the organization – not merely shared accountability authority-line exposure. Something changes in a person who has ultimate and final accountability for something, versus an individual who merely participates or shares accountability for substantive issues.

7. **Researched and/or published in the areas that an organization is engaged in** also aids in the shaping of critical 'thought capacity' and the focusing of thought for public consumption via print or oral arenas. This does not include mere busy-work activities, but rather real substantive actions.

8. **Crises or high-demand (pressure, conflict, confrontational, etc.) participation** and survival outcome activities, either in personal or professional environments, will provide functional experience that will prove valuable for objective and critical 'thought capacity.'

9. **Normal or routine operational line and leadership position participation** with high-level measurable and quantifiable productivity in each of the essential functional areas of an organization (or they bring an equivalent from a parallel environment that would be transferable and applicable).

10. **Disaster and failure lessons learned.** What does the person need to have experienced, relevant to your organization and market, which cannot afford to be repeated? These are quite often the most valuable 'experiences' that shape powerful 'thought leader capacity' for an individual.

When you observe the costly poor decisions implemented by individuals or organizations (watch your local news for examples with military leaders and organizational leaders, or listen to those around you talk about their colleagues . . .), ask yourself how many of the above action areas may have been lacking in that individual or organization.

"Most people are really defined by what they won't compromise on, more so than what they will compromise on!"
- Charles Sweatt, Retired, Sergeant Major, US ARMY

Many people mean well, but they have been conditioned by their environment and the people that have touched their lives and denied the 'experiences' necessary to grow great 'thought leaders' for the future!

"A man without decision can never be said to belong to himself."
- John Foster

Chapter EIGHT
Developing Thought Leader Capacity: Model of Replication

"It is not a question how much a man knows, but what use he makes of what he knows. Not a question of what he has acquired and how he has been trained, but of what he is and what he can do."
- J. G. Holland

A 'thought leader's' capacity to think independently and objectively is essential in facilitating decisions in an effective manner, whether under pressure, in the midst of a crises or entirely free of pressure . . . .

A systematic decision matrix I developed for IBM many years ago is a powerful template for 'thought leaders' to use in facilitating sound decision-making today. There tend to be three distinct derailment zones, which can kill free flowing 'thought processes':

1. Procrastination – born out of one's inability to clearly see an issue, situation, or stimulant.

2. Paralysis-of-Analysis – born out of a need to over-analyze or study.

3. Fear – born out of a feeling of a lack of sound data from which to make a decision, concern about the ramifications of a decision, etc.

To address these derailment zones, stimulate forward movement as a 'thought leader', and avoid costly debates with others, one can facilitate the decision process and feed free flowing 'thought processes' by using the "**STOP Model**!"

Part of effective 'thought leader' ability comes from an ability to facilitate the basic decision-making process. There are four basic steps to effective decision-making:

1. **(S) Stop and See** precisely what the challenge, problem, need, or subject matter for discussion is. From the first step, one's ability to singularly see the "what factor" will guide them to the second step of the decision making process because there will no longer be a need to participate in step one activity.

2. **(T) Target and Think** precisely why that matter has been raised and why it is worthy of your time and investment of mental energy to determine the basis for its analysis. Once there is an understanding of the "why factor" by you, and all other vested parties, for this subject to be addressed, move onward to step three. It is during this vital step two that one often becomes disproportionately sidetracked. Thus effective 'thought processes' become derailed.

3. **(O) Organize Options** according to the best way to proceed. This step directs you to invest your mental energies, and those of those around you, to explore and brainstorm viable solutions and options to each item you have selected to run through the four-step

model. This step is also critical for effective 'thought leader' development, as this step serves as an insurance policy, which dictates that no action be initiated unless there are at least two viable options from which to select. This will ensure that, as a 'thought leader,' you have a contingency plan in case the first application solution fails.

4. **(P) Pick and Proceed** with that option which is most viable. As a 'thought leader' you will now be able to always focus on the decision process with the end always foremost in your mind.

As a 'thought leader', one will be armed with a powerful self-management tool that will allow for the replication of effective, consistent decision-making to take place. The **"STOP Model"** also affords managerial-leaders an objective instrument for cultivating involvement from a cross section of personalities in the pursuit of stimulating open 'thought processes' organizationally for lasting success!

"I find the great thing in this world is not so much where we stand, as in what direction we are moving."
Oliver Wendell Holmes

SECTION THREE:
Motivating

Chapter 9   Motivating The Individual
                 Within
Chapter 10   Motivating The Team With
                 Which You Connect
Chapter 11   Motivating Oneself
Chapter 12   Motivating Relationships
                 Together

Chapter NINE
Motivating the Individual Within

"The world belongs to the energetic."
- Ralph Waldo Emerson

Recognizing performance 'well done' is an accomplishment in many different ways from a managerial-leadership perspective.

Cultivating energies and dedication from an organization's bench is essential. Whether done as incentives, bonus systems, perks, recognition initiatives, or whatever else, the act of motivating one from their perspective is the equivalent to a new tank of gasoline in an automobile.

One of the traps, which management has evolved into over past decades, is the belief that all people are motivated in the same manner. In actuality, surveys reveal that what may be a motivator for one individual, may, in fact, be a de-motivator for another.

Management and personnel experts invest a tremendous amount of energy to determine what works and what doesn't. Research detailed in *YIELD MANAGEMENT: The Leadership Alternative for Performance and Net Profit Improvement*®*!* (By CRC Press, ISBN# 1-57444-206-6 / USA $29.95) illustrates that most of what has been done has been a complete waste of everyone's time.

For any motivator to have real impact, there are three guideposts that must be adhered to first:

1. The act or gesture must be of **meaning** to the specific recipient, regardless of applicability to others.

2. The act or gesture must be **repeatable** . . . what do you do for the next accomplishment which warrants recognition?

3. The act or gesture must be of such nature that there is some degree of **lasting impact** . . . something that won't lose its meaning the next day!

    By rewarding the desired behavior and net results of a star player on your bench in a meaningful way, that player will be psychologically and subconsciously reminded of the reward every time they do a similar future act.

Here is a fast track formula that we have found, amazingly, always works with our Fortune 100 clients and governmental agency leaders, when determining what works and what doesn't with every employee within an organization.

While occasionally there may be some environments that have become stagnant due to the acceptance of institutional mediocrity, the following is a great process for determining what works:

1. Have each employee or direct report on your bench complete a **"self-motivator assessment sheet"** or profile. Instruct them to detail as many responses as appropriate for/to themselves under two headers or categories; keep it in your personnel files for future reference.

2. Have each employee list those things that, to them, would be appreciated acts or gestures from management. Instruct them to organize their lsts into two categories: **'FREE'** and **'FINANCIAL,'** for acts with cost perimeters about them.

The beauty of this sheet is that the "self-motivator assessments" allow managerial-leaders to ensure that every time **meaning** is attained, the actions are easily **repeatable**. Because the actions are coming from the recipient's inventory, **lasting impact** is more often attainable.

This simple three-step formula is incredibly powerful in today's work place, as studies have determined that individuals are motivated in professional environments in one of three core ways:

1. By 'Self Fulfillment' acts.
2. By 'Recognition' delivered in a variety of ways.
3. By 'Intrinsic' motives.

Using the above two templates, managerial-leaders in today's high speed, results-oriented environments can increase their ability to connect with individuals and motivate each individual from within his or her own rulebook of what matters!

"No man who continues to add something to the material, intellectual,
and moral well being of the place in which he lives
is left long without proper reward."
- Booker T. Washington

Chapter TEN
Motivating the Team With Which You Connect

"Each man should frame life so that, at some future hour,
fact and his dreamings meet."
- Victor Hugo

The days of 'one approach serves all' for recognizing and motivating groups of people in the work place have long gone. Due, in large part, to the melding of work force environments, comprised of diverse cultures, gender mixes, wide ranging generational segmentations, race, differing levels of work sophistication and tenure, a more precise connection is required.

In studying group dynamics, there are six specific ways that managerial-leaders can connect and motivate groups of people today. The greater the opportunity for a leader to connect on multiple levels, the greater the sense of appreciation will be by individuals, and, thus, a sense of belonging and participation will build among all members. Indirectly and directly these acts will serve to motivate the overall team or work group.

Recognizing opportunities to allow individuals and groups to perform can either make being in management a joy and honor or a complete nightmare! For management, finding those rare connection points becomes an opportunity to truly motivate and inspire greatness in a group, as if they were one entity.

Our studies indicate that six common threads to which management can look, thereby **"Intrinsically Motivating The Team,"** are:

Choice – When opportunities allow for an
individual or small grouping of members of a team, department, or work group to make independent 'choices' from the range of **"WHAT"** factors . . . in essence, when one is allowed to select their own task, a significantly higher level of energy, commitment, creativity, and dedication will be
demonstrated.

Decision – Allowing individuals to exercise their own ability to 'decide' exactly **"HOW"** to execute a game plan will also yield significantly greater outcomes. To determine when to intervene and when to withdraw from **"HOW"** someone is to implement their game plan, reflect on three core issues: Legality, Ethics, and Cost Effectiveness. If their action plan is legal, ethical, and cost effective, and so is yours, let them do it their way. If any of these three issues are in conflict, however, and it must be your way, speak solely to that element.

Creativity – Make the work environment a safe environment for individuals to bring their creative self to play and allow for maximum ownership.

Feedback – Immediately afterwards, provide
individuals with constructive feedback that is fair, unbiased, and action-plan oriented. This will feed their energized soul.

Challenge – Individuals within a group must be realistically 'challenged' in their performance. Studies by insurance companies and the Federal Government indicate the highest level of on-the-job accidents and injuries occurs in those places where people become complacent and unchallenged. This allows people to become mentally disengaged from their work, resulting in the decline of productivity, enthusiasm, and motivation.

Competition – The laws of competitive nature reveal that there are three ways in which an individual and group of people pull together and work enthusiastically as one unit. We can be motivated forward when 'compelled' by 'competing' against "Someone Else," "Something Else," or "Our Self"!

An ability to motivate the teams one leads and the teams one is a part of is a true sign of managerial-leadership greatness. Attaining this level of effectiveness will serve to be a continued source of team motivation . . . that which excites us serves as petroleum in our gas tank of human life!

"Success is held in the journey and not the destination.
Notice what one learns from the journey and how to
replicate that as often as possible!"
- Jeff Magee

Chapter ELEVEN
Motivating Oneself For Sustained Peak Performance

"Nothing in this world is so good as usefulness. It binds your fellow creatures to you and you to them. It tends to the improvement of your own character and gives you a real importance in society much beyond what any artificial station can bestow."
- B. C. Brodie

Motivating those on one's team for peak performance and sustained performance ability is essential to a healthy organization. At the same time, leaders must be always vigilant to remain energized and motivated themselves if they want their team to demonstrate similar traits and characteristics.

A mentor of mine once expressed the view that if organizations hired motivated people, they would be able to spend less time focusing on how to motivate and reward employees.

While I agree to that statement in spirit, I do feel that the individuals' sustained acts that are recognized and appreciated serve as ongoing fuel in one's gas tank of life. If one puts out energy without being replenished, one will ultimately burn out and crash!

Here are ten simple proven strategies for remaining energized and motivated in the work place as a managerial-leader. Consider:

1. **Completion** – Psychology reveals that one's mind must see completion or accomplishment to energy expanded. If one works on project(s), and, at the end of the day, nothing quantifiable is accomplished, it becomes harder and harder to sustain that same level, not mention an increased level, of commitment and enthusiasm toward the project. It is natural for the mind to divert energies toward other matters when it does not see results. So, a simple,yet meaningful example would be to make sure that every day your schedule is loaded with something that you can look back upon at the end of the day as having accomplished, a this or a that.

2. **Limit Exposure To People** – Limit the amount of time you spend around those people that are 'takers' and not 'givers' of energy. Engaging individuals that tend to be energy drainers, negative perspective-oriented, and toxic personalities are sure-fire ways of having energy drained from you. Have a strategy for engaging them that allows you to engage and escape quickly. As detailed in *ENOUGH ALREADY: 50 Fast Ways To Deal With, Manage And Eliminate Negativity At Work And Home*®, I have found that by limiting your exposure to these types of people you will remain motivated and willing volunteered and subjected themselves to an event or group of people. This self-inflicted energy-robbing experience can be greatly curtailed by reducing, and sometimes eliminating, one's willingness to be placed in these scenarios! In his landmark book, *You Don't Have To Be Blind To See*®, Jim Stovall demonstrates

repeatedly that the greatest obstacles to success and motivation are self- inflicted!

3. **Personal Mission Statement Focus** – Individuals with defined self purpose, as Stephen Covey called it in his best selling book, The *7 Habits Of Highly Effective People*®, are in fact successful and live in greater self harmony because they gravitate toward those things and people that have connection with what they are about. This serves as a self- fulfilling energy depositor.

4. **Professional Mission Statement Focus** – so too would hold true for truly effective professionals. They arrive in the work place with clarity of purpose that holds self- meaning, and when engaged in actions that serve this purpose, they too seem to become more energized and motivated.

5. **Master Mind Group** – Famed businessman of the mid 1900's, Napoleon Hill, in the classic book, *Success Through A Positive Mental Attitude*®, called it one's personal board-of-directors. To surround yourself with like professionals that you can draw upon for open, candid, and confidential input in times of high and low will be a powerful personal force. Your Master Mind Group will serve as a constant source of inspiration and motivation to you and your causes.

6. **Other Person Focused** – Whether referred to as servant leadership or customer focused, when you understand what is held to be truly meaningful to the other person in the work place, and you can assist them in attaining that, you will find them to

be a more willing participant in your circles. This willingness feeds your energy, and the two of you become more moved, motivated, and energized!

7. **Limit Exposure To Things** – Limit the amount of time you spend on projects, activities, committees, or things that are 'takers' and not 'givers' of energy. Participating in some of those 'things' that one does not always have to engage in, tend to be energy drainers of you. Have a strategy that will tell you when to engage and participate and when to bite your tongue, shut up, and or not even show up to the event! You will find that by limiting your exposure to these types of 'things,' you will remain motivated and energized more often.

8. **Don't Volunteer** – It is amazing to listen to your self-talk at those times when you feel abused, taken advantage of, not appreciated, etc., and realize that for a large percentage of the time, this occurs when one has actions; energies are working together and not against one another!

9. **Don't Argue** – Without question, the fastest way to drain one's energy level, increase one's negative self-talk, and reduce forward momentum both in the now and contribute to possible future obstacles, is to engage in an argument with another person in a professional environment. Just recognize that, in most arguments, there are two critical questions: Who gets exhausted? Who gets energized? This will aid as a good guidepost toward future engagements for sustained enthusiasm.

10. Just Do It – As the mantra goes, so to do winners! Procrastination and the act of 'excuse- it is' can hold one back from victory. Victories serve as energy depositors; the act of waiting, holding back, putting off, and just simple procrastination on those tasks, issues, etc., which one must address only serves to be powerful demotivators. It is like building a daily 'to do' list and putting the ugly task as last. It only serves to ruin an otherwise great day and will ensure that you go about that matter with only half your energy level. Load that type of activity into the day after some thing great and before something great, and even it will be done with great motivation. And as a leader, you must remember your team 'models' the behaviors they see exhibited from you

Unlocking the door to one's passion points has a dramatic effect of becoming a never-ending waterfall from which one gains a flow of energy. It is from this flow of energy, which serves as the core source of one's energy creators, that one will be able to sustain constant motivation.

As a leader it is you that serves as the well to which the team comes for nurturing and substance!

Chapter TWELVE
Motivating Relationships Together

"The greatest single thing in the qualification of a great player, a great team, or a great man is a desire to reach the objective that admits of no interference anywhere."
- Branch Rickey

Have you ever wondered what really makes a relationship with another person work? How about what it takes to cultivate and maintain healthy relationships, with those that one works with, for sustained commitment and motivation by all parties?

Well, the reverse may be easier to answer. And from that new understanding, a managerial-leader can begin to build the framework around which people can come together to work more effectively and connect with one another more constructively in a motivated manner.

As one of the youngest Certified Management Consultants (CMC) today, working with organizations internationally, I have found that there are two sure fire ways for individuals within an organization to self-destruct and thereby erode the potential of healthy working relationships from ever developing. Organizational psychologists – whose results have coincided with personal therapists' findings with couples – have found the most prevalent reasons for this dysfunction. People tend to have conflict with one another or have difficulty connecting with others for two primary reasons:

1. *The individuals involved in a conflict are so similar* that they don't see the difficulty in the other person as being precisely what they are exhibiting themselves.

2. The individuals, who are involved in the conflict or having a difficult time creating a healthy working relationship with one another, *really don't know and, thus, don't understand one another.*

To develop healthy relationships in the work place that feed collaboration, unity, energy, and motivation, consider the four basic sides to what we have found to be essential ingredients for a successful relationship – at home and in business. To build healthy relationships, concentrate as a managerial- leader to ask, "What are the differing 'acts' that one can exhibit or engage in that create, reinforce, or foster the four sides to actualize?"

Consider motivated relationships in a work environment as an imaginary *"Relationship Cube©."* Each side is critical to holding a healthy relationship together. Visualize a cube with four labeled sides:

TRUST

MOTIVATION		ASSERTIVENESS

COMMUNICATION

These 'acts' that allow each side of this *"Relationship Cube©"* to stand solid, are the answer to effective managerial- leadership today within an organization. As a leader, what you are also tasked with and own is the responsibility to channel some of your energy into cultivating future leaders from within your organization by forging healthy motivated relationships with them.

The four fastest 'acts' that I have seen that aid the four sides in maturing relationships to a level of motivation for one another, and, at the same time, are the four fastest ways to implode a relationship are:

1. **TRUST** – Be an example of *"honesty"* among others. People today are born with innate "BS" meters. They can detect untruths and deception, and will recall for eternity betrayal.

2. **ASSERTIVENESS** – Allow everyone to share their *"opinions"* as long as they are even remotely close to the issues and subjects at hand. To shut down people's 'opinions' is almost an assured way to kill off the asserted behaviors most needed in a healthy work place.

3. **MOTIVATION** - Dispense a genuine, sincere *"Thank You"* to those on your team.

4. **COMMUNICATION** – People will sense if you are being *"Open, Fai,r and Consistent"* in your pursuit of sending and receiving communication signals with all those around you.

The act of cultivating motivated relationships with others on a team is essential to sustained success and efficiency within an organization. When a lack of healthy motivated relationships are allowed to develop, an organization will experience attrition, peak performers leaving for the competition or worse yet, the further splitting of the business pie by exiting members of an organization, who leave and create their own competing business entity.

> *"Successful people should be confident enough with themselves to share openly of themselves with others, so as to render themselves obsolete in pursuit of developing others fully."*
> *- David Small*
> *(shared via a story he learned from his college mentor)*

In fact, Marcus Buckingham, a global practice leader with the Gallup Organization, spent the past decade surveying more than 2.5 million employees to determine key factor determinates in how engaged an employee will become in an organization and what causes that involvement. Of the survey questions, three critical factors surfaced from the employees' perspective:

1. Do I know what is expected of me at work?
2. Do I have an opportunity to do what I do best every day?
3. Does my supervisor or someone at work care about me?

A leader's ability to foster and promote healthy relations with individuals and groups in the work place will feed constructive response to these three questions. In fact, when there is the existence of a solid *"Relationship Cube©,"* individuals will become engaged in an organization, and passions, motivation, and commitment will surface for an overall motivated group!

SECTION FOUR:
Building Political Capital

Chapter 13	Building Political Capital: One Partnership "Decision" at a Time
Chapter 14	Building Political Capital: Selecting Fast Partners Via "Rule 80-10-10"
Chapter 15	Building Political Capital: "Deposits" and "Withdrawals" to Relationships
Chapter 16	Building Political Capital: Saving Face and Bouncing Back From Controversy

Chapter THIRTEEN
Building Political Capital:
One Partnership "Decision" At
A Time

"Don't accept superficial solutions for difficult problems."
- Bertrand Russell

The adages abound: '*together everyone achieves more*' (team), there is no *"I"* in the word '*we,*' '*whether you think you can or you think you cannot, you are correct*' (a.k.a. Henry Fordism)…

Strategically building alliances, coalitions, or partnerships as one ascends professionally is good political sense. Doing so in a manner that aids both immediate needs and aligns with long-term goals is the tricky science!

How one goes about building their personal and professional political capital plays a critical role in both how hard one works and how far one ascends within an organization, industry, and life. These actions also play into the chemistry of future interpersonal relationships with those around you – positively and negatively. Here are some considerations for building political capital via your partnerships.

Consideration One: In building one's political capital, always *ensure that any short-term decisions or associations do not adversely impact one's long-term needs.* Far too often, people make immediate decisions to address an immediate need without considering the implication of that decision on long-term needs or expectations.

Consideration Two: *Guilt by association complex.* Consider the association that you are about to forge from an objective second party perspective. How do others, especially other influencers and key stakeholders, view the individual or group that you are about to engage? Contemplate how to address any negative fallout from others, if you were to go forward with that partnership for an immediate need or long term need, if there were to be controversy or negativity associated with it.

Consideration Three: *Examine each relational decision as to how it will influence other decisions.* Explore how every decision will subsequently influence or impact all other parallel decisions being made and future decisions and action plans needing to be implemented. This "forward thinking" allows you to look at each decision from a "reverse thinking" perspective before it is made. For example:

1. Take two pieces of string, about twelve inches long, and tack one end down on a surface.

2. Now move one string about two inches outward in any direction from where it is anchored down; tack that down.

3. Next, take the second piece of string and move it outward in the same direction, making that string a very slight distance left or right of the first one. Go outward about the same two inches and tack it down.

4. Examine the two strings. They start off in the same place and both go outward the same distance. One is going to be just slightly askew from the other at this two-inch point. Correct?

5. Take both strings and their remaining 10 inches and continue both outward on the same path that they are on at the two-inch point. Tack each down where they end.

6. Now examine how a slight change or difference in decision at the beginning only slightly impacts the location at the two-inch point. Notice that with a slight corrective decision at that point you can get both strings back together. However, at the twelve-inch point, there is an obvious distance between the two strings, and it would take measurable course correction to get the two strings to come back together.

The point is powerful. While many immediate decisions may not be recognized as having lasting influence and effect on where one ultimately ends up in life, every decision does have a relational influence on one's end-point!

Consideration Four: *Three cornerstones to most decisions.* If one visualizes a triangle and labels each side – one "Cost/Financial", one "Time/Efficiency", and one "Quality" – then one can weigh the associated factors to a decision and whether a partnership is warranted, and, if so, how that partnership will impact the overall decision.

The desired balance between these three elements is the ultimate goal in selecting your partnerships that add to, and not take away from, one's political capital. However, many times a decision has to forgo one of these sides at the expense of the other. So always ask yourself if you gain on one side, which other side pays the price? Can you afford the short-term and long-term results of that decision?

Explore how you must negotiate with that potential partner the compensation variables for what is gained and what is lost in your decision process. Also, discuss (or at least contemplate personally) how one will participate with the other on decisions, when you must forgo one variable at the expense of another. Ask yourself what "leverage" you will have now and in the future to compel that other party to honor those future commitments made in the present tense. Human nature is such that, without leverage (positive or negative), people tend not to change or act in your desired expectations.

These are merely some of the critical considerations one should evaluate in building alliances, coalitions, or partnerships strategically and in building political capital that can be drawn upon for leverage and success – both professionally and personally.

Chapter *FOURTEEN*
Building Political Capital:
Selecting Fast Partners Via
"Rule 80-10-10©"

Many times your political clout is determined by the alliances you keep. To build fast coalitions, look at the groups you engage and make the choice to select that subgroup or individual with whom you have the greatest connection or possible connection.

> *"The fact that I always have a choice was one*
> *of the most illuminating and liberating concepts*
> *that I ever learned. I realized that I may not always*
> *like the choices, but I always have a choice."*

Profound words from, The Spirituality of Success: Getting Rich With Integrity® (ISBN#0-9706988-7-9 / US $16.95) by Vincent Roazzi, a colleague with whom I have had valuable dialogue on this matter of building political capital through strategic partnerships within an organization.

Demographers typically break groups down into three subgroups. I refer to these three subgroups, which comprise every large group in which you engage or participate, as "Followers" of the influencers to the overall group, forward moving "Transformers", and negative, reverse moving "Terrorists!"

Most groups tend to subdivide, classifying 80 percent as "Followers", 10 percent as "Transformers", and 10 percent as "Terrorists" – hence, you can build your political capital faster by deploying "Rule 80-10-10".

It is not until either one of the influencer subgroups gains momentum that the "Followers" fall in behind them. If this energy is counter to your position, not only will there be formidable energy counter to you, but it will also be very difficult for anyone to go public in favor of you – regardless of how valid your positions may be. You have, at this point, seemingly no political capital to rally to your cause, nor do you have any political capital behind you.

To avoid these nightmarish scenarios, consider how you can pre-engage each group. To quickly gain political capital, look at every engagement with a group objectively and consider that every personality within that group can become very fluid and move from one subgroup to another, based upon the overall mix of personalities and/or the issue at hand on any given occasion.

There are two basic ways that you can deploy to build your political capital and draw in support from your "Transformer" base. This effort will aid and most often ensure the support of their constituent, the "Followers".

When engaging any group, you can determine who your candidates for "Transformers" are by asking:

1. Who do I know best among this group? Who likes me? Who do I like? Who owes me a favor?
2. Who has the most to gain by endorsing this idea that I have? Who has the most to loose if this idea does not go through?

With this determination made, engage these people offline and discuss with them what it is that you want to accomplish when you engage the overall group. Solicit their feedback on your ideas. You may need to be flexible at this point in order to adopt some of their thinking into your idea and gain their support and endorsement. When you engage the overall group, you can conversationally name-drop those with whom you have had the pleasure of dialoguing beforehand and that "they 'like the idea,' so let me present it to everyone now". "Terrorists," sensing that you have a support network, will be exceedingly resistant in attacking.

Smart cultivation of your political capital and the strategic use of that political capital will typically ensure greater gains and success. As you gain more successes in these endeavors, momentum is built in-and-of-itself, and further increases your political power, influence, and celebrity standing among and over groups in which you move.

The continued use of your political power and political capital for the well being of those around you will further enhance your political capital. Conversely, you can over-draw your political capital reserves if you become too self-serving!

What will sabotage this effort? Most people tend to defend their views and represent their views when challenged by others. Do not do this, as it plays to the "Terrorists" and typically makes you look ineffective. This becomes compounded by the fact that the "Followers" will then begin to fall in behind the "Terrorists," as their views will seem louder and more plausible than yours. The final blow comes as you continue to defend and re-justify. You realize that what remaining "Transformers" there might have been will not rally behind you – you are all alone!

By using **"Rule 80-10-10©"** you can determine your best candidates for "Transformers" and "Followers," and ,thus, neutralizers to "Terrorists," in building to your political capital within the organizations that you serve for greater organizational yield!

"Every person is responsible for all the good within the
scope of his abilities and for no more; and none can tell
whose sphere is the largest"
- Gail Hamilton

Chapter FIFTEEN
Building Political Capital: The Necessary "Deposits" and "Withdrawals" to Relationship Building!

"It is perfectly true, as philosophers say, that life must be understood backwards. But they forget the other proposition, that it must be lived forwards."
- Soren Kierkegaard, Philosopher

In building one's political capital, it is necessary to examine each relationship individually and on the merits of that relationship, in respect to what one does to build and foster the relationship.

View each relationship that you forge as a financial account. Consider how much you invest into the other party, how often you put something constructive into that relationship, and what you do to grow that relationship as "Deposits." Conversely, be conscious of everything that you do as a direct and indirect action that can be seen as a "Withdrawal" from that relationship.

Your political capital and spendable political capital will come from those accounts in which you have significant vested interest – "Deposits!"

These **"Deposits"** can be made in many different ways. Consider the following:

1. Immediate professional functional position deposits that aid what they do daily. Be consistent and repetitive in these actions . . . it will be the compounding interest of these net actions that will make the biggest influence.

2. Professional deposits that advance their job, department, team, division, or work unit that will raise their stock value (worth to others) in other people's eyes.

3. Advancing a cause in their work place that they hold very personal and important professionally.

4. Providing assistance to someone at work they respect greatly and/or are mentoring.

5. Aiding a personal cause (directly or indirectly) that they publicly champion.

6. Availing yourself openly to them when they need you, and maintaining strictness of confidences.

7. Standing with them at a critical time, when others are abandoning them and the cause would have little adverse impact on your core political support system and personal goals.

Conversely, **"Withdrawals"** can be made in many different ways. Consider:

1. The opposite of any of the individual "Deposits" can create an imbalance.

2. Having opinions shaped by daily census trends or polls, regardless of the big picture, can create very transparent political capital networks and actually serve to bitter key stakeholders toward you in the medium and long-term time frames.

3. Waffling on core purposes or beliefs, to an organization or the other party's professional domain, can create a "withdrawal" scenario with the political capital you are courting, cultivating, or attempting to grow.

4. Any threat or perceived threat to the interpersonal relationship between you or the other party's circle of influence.

In the end, visualize each relationship as if it were based upon a teeter-totter analogy. The base of that image is the relationship name, and the plank that would be placed on top of it has a "Deposit" or Plus Sign on one side and a "Withdrawal" or Negative-Sign on the other. Ask yourself which way the plank is leaning, and that will give you a quick visualization of whether or not you have spendable political capital.

Seldom do people have relationships (or at least sustainable long-term relationships) that will afford them spendable political capital. When the teeter-totter of any individual relationship leans in a negative direction, you are losing your political capital. As in the financial world, one can have 'over-draft protection' to guard them against making an unexpected 'Withdrawal" when there are no "Deposits" there to facilitate the transaction.

"The greatest men in all ages have been lovers of their kind. All true leaders of men have it. Faith in men and regard for men are unfailing marks of true greatness."
- Ralph Waldo Emerson

Chapter SIXTEEN
Building Political Capital:
The ABC's of Saving Face and
Bouncing Back From Controversy

"Those who are quite satisfied, sit still and do nothing;
those who are not quite satisfied are the sole benefactors of
the world."
- Landor

Many rising stars have burned out of control and, thus, been denied the opportunity to shine. This is due to experiencing a miss-step in action or words, and not bouncing back quickly enough to save their political capital. As a leader, what will speak volumes about your leadership capacity will not be if you have a miss-step, but how you handle your miss-steps.

The efficient first steps, after one finds him or herself in a controversy, are critical to saving face and moving forward quickly. How one publicly handles the miss-step, and how one privately, tactically deploys his or her political capital, will mean the literal difference between success and stress.

Consider a simple "ABC Approach" to bouncing back from controversy and ensuring no loss of political capital:

1. **Act** – Immediately to ACTION! Don't wait and place yourself in a position of responding (logic-based behaviors) or reacting (emotion-based behaviors) to others. Take control of your destiny

and remember that even a decision not to act is, in effect, an act of action

2. **Blitz** – Immediately, go behind the scenes, one-on-one, and build support from your political advocates, stakeholders, mentors, and champions. Address each one individually and communicate your position, your apology for the miss step and any unpleasantness it has brought to them.

   Ask for his or her 'advice' on the best way to proceed and put this event behind everyone. Explore sincere and powerful ways to direct the attention coming to you onto another meaningful issue. In essence, you want to brainstorm ways to capitalize upon the limited attention directed toward you, blend with it, and direct that attention and energy in a more constructive direction.

   Solicit feedback from these people as to how they can play an active role, either publicly or privately, to curtail the negative press, eliminate or quiet any impending lynch mobs, and assist in repairing any wounds to your political capital net worth

3. **Communicate** – Make a conscious and purposeful public statement (whatever that means to your environment) that addresses the intent upon which you want people to focus and the miss-deed that has created the immediate controversy. The longer you wait to communicate, the more people will fill in the lack of communication with speculation and gossip. Once this happens, the initial miss-step takes on a life of its own and becomes even more difficult to personally address. It can create a

climate, where your political capital may erode before your very eyes!

Bouncing back from situational controversies and saving political face are critical to professional success and the overall leadership effectiveness that one will experience.

This "ABC Approach" has been well constructed and used across the spectrum of professional, personal, and even political stages.

For example, notice how easily people's attention can be swayed from real issues to superficial issues, and how long-standing self-centered individuals thrive. The best laboratory for viewing this is through our evening news, and how they portray national political figures of any party ... "deflect, deny and denigrate" is their motto. And their lasting political capital is zero, as their political capital is merely situational to their present position. When they leave it, their lives become very shallow and empty, as controversies of the long past remain hung around their necks forever.

Build your political capital by genuinely investing in others in your organizations, as if you were going to live with them for the remainder of your days. Then you will find a different behavior approach to your every action!

SECTION FIVE:
Independent Thought

Chapter 17   Independent   Thought:
                  Assuming   Self-Accountability
                  With Integrity
Chapter 18   Independent   Thought:
                  Sustaining a Lonely Position
Chapter 19   Independent Thought:
                  Weathering the Storm of
                  Criticism

Chapter SEVENTEEN
Independent Thought:
Assuming Self-Accountability as a Leader and Doing So With Integrity!

"When we have practiced good actions a while, they become easy; when they are easy we take pleasure in them; when they please us we do them frequently; and then, by frequency of act, they grow into habit."
- Tillotson

It could be said that one's "integrity" (ethics being the root of one's integrity) is what guides one's decisions and actions when no one is around to witness what one does!

Countless managers never ascend to the ranks of effective or great leaders for a host of reasons. Topping that list would be their inability to practice "independent thought" as the catalyst to independent actions. One's inability to think independently is systemic of a host of personal and organizational problems gone awry today.

A cancer attacking leaders within organizations and society today is the apparent lack of individuals' ability to think independently. With many high profile individuals, they repeatedly demonstrate the new fashion plate of shallow leadership as having to tap into opinion polls, survey data, or census samplings for the basis to what their views should be. Thus their subsequent decisions and actions are gauged accordingly. CNN will typically survey 100-to-200

Americans and run that information as a "Survey-of-Americans say ... !"

This is reinforced in today's workplace and society by a seemingly fashionable desire to abdicate decisions and self-responsibility. This behavior appears to be accepted by a host of psychologists, who can explain away actions, and championed by a line of lawyers, who are willing to litigate that fact and lay the burden of blame at the feet of someone else!

Today, endless studies of successful people amazingly reveal one consistent denominator, which continually gets overlooked – the studied successful individuals have both the ability to "Think Independently" and take action!

As a leader, it is paramount that one is able and willing to think independently when necessary. Consider the great words of U.S. President Calvin Coolidge (1872):

*"Nothing in the world can take the place of persistence.
Talent will not; nothing is more common than
unsuccessful men with talent. Genius will not;
unrewarded genius is almost a proverb.
Education will not; the world is full of educated failures.
Persistence and determination alone are omnipotent.
Press on!"*

In assuming self-accountability, without the need of someone else making the decisions for you or having someone rubber-stamp your thoughts prior to acting upon them, consider the following protocols:

1. Have a clearly defined personal and professional mission statement. This will serve as a guidepost for

actions one should take, must take, and not take. The drill of drafting such a statement will bring extreme clarity to your purpose and place meaning where you need it most!

2. Understand the core purpose to the organization that one serves and use this as a benchmark in guiding all thought processes. This will further drive your actions when others are present and when you are by yourself.

   For example: This will aid you especially well in meetings or "group think" sessions, when the impending thoughts that are about to drive decisions will cause damage to the well being of the organization. You can break out from the crowd and be confident to rise to the level of expressing your independent thoughts.

3. Recognize the depth of your political capital/network within your organization and the level of support that you can expect from them, based upon your thoughtful decisions.

4. Ask yourself if the "gain" or "loss" to making no decision would be such that, weighed against the status quo, you should be compelled to make a decision now – regardless to what others may think.

5. Contemplate issues objectively and independently of other issues, based upon your "Technical/Educational," "Prior Performance," "Experience", and "Certification" levels. As you dig within yourself for answers, based upon these tangibles, proceed based upon evidence and sound

logic. If you are out of your depth, access those around you, who could serve as situational subject matter experts.

Assuming self-accountability to making independent decisions is a hallmark to independent thought that leads one to greatness and gives cause to others to want to rally behind you!

Chapter EIGHTEEN
Independent Thought:
Making a Decision and Sustaining It as a Lonely Position!

"Fortunate is the person who has developed the self-control to steer a straight course toward his objective ... "
- Napoleon Hill

Some say making an independent thought actualize without a cheering crowd of support is among the loneliest of positions.

To maintain your professional focus as a leader and sustain that metal of steadiness, when seemingly no one around you wants to participate in the decision process or rally energy around you for making a decision, consider:

1. Is the decision congruent with what the organization stands for? If so, be resolute and move onward.

2. As the managerial-leader, while most will not publicly voice their support for you, they do, in fact, support you and value your presence. Demographers indicate that up to 80 percent of individuals won't outwardly express independent thought; they will merely channel their energies in the direction which they feel is most accepted by the overall organization, environment, or leadership. Smile internally with that knowledge.

3. Have a support network, removed from your work environment (mentor, advisor, performance coach, etc.), to which you can consult before, during, and after independent thought activities have been actualized.

4. Reflect upon the decision and the endpoint, as long as the application of your thought is taking you toward that endpoint. Don't let the intermediate, and often temporary, pressures during implementation drive you off course or hamper future self-initiative.

5. Maintain thorough communication with participants in the execution of any decision, and keep a free flow of communication among active participants. This will aid in giving you confidence and peace of mind at any given time. This act will also serve to encourage others to support your decisions and work to stifle any counter communications, as a result of a lack of communication.

Making an independent decision as a leader and sustaining that decision and your demeanor can be a lonely position.

That loneliness can be transformed into a source of energy and commitment to one's professionalism, once it is realized that "Independent Thought" is not fashionable among the masses, and people do, in fact, hunger for that rare individual with the capacity to perform. A manager can follow procedures and policies; a leader knows when and how to stand out from the rest and enjoy the moments of solitude, which forecast opportunities for even greater windows of "independent thought!"

*"Living truth is that alone which has its origin in thinking.
Just as a tree bears, year after year, the same fruit, and yet
fruit, which is each year new, so must all permanently
valuable ideas be continually born again in thought."*
- Albert Schweitzer

Chapter NINETEEN
Independent Thought:
Weathering the Storm Of Criticism!

"Your personal 'quest for excellence' can be another way
of saying 'my character is showing.'"
- Earl Nightingale

The weather is always quietest before the storm!

So goes the adage of time. So too is the relevance of recognizing that when you, as a leader, dare to venture off the beaten path with a decision that smacks against conventional thought, the calm immediately after making an independent thought may, in fact, be the precursor to a storm of criticism.

At this point, you should realize that you can engage the storm-makers in one of three ways:

1. **You can attempt to ignore, as most managers would choose.** This only manifests into a larger problem, when the subtleties of the storm grow into a hurricane of public criticism, and otherwise still individuals become vocal resisters to your initiatives.

2. **You can challenge and get pulled into the debate of defending ones' position, as an inexperienced individual would do.** This is almost sure to cause your emotions to erupt in the presence of the other

party's seemingly calm logic, thus reducing you to a dark cloud in everyone else's estimation.

3. **<u>You can engage, which is how a leader would facilitate the scenario.</u>** There are a host of constructive engagement strategies and tactics that a leader can deploy at this point.

The critical element at the onset of a storm is to position yourself to work with the approaching energy force and utilize it to your advantage.

One way to do this is to **"Demand an Alternative!"** At the precise moment someone criticizes your thoughts, decisions, and actions, calmly look at them and politely ask, *"If this idea is not the most effective way to approach this matter, what would you feel to be a more effective way to address it?"*

If they cannot put forth a constructive response (many times your retort will catch them off guard, and they will most likely respond by saying something like, "because" – a response that is to be completely accepted, not scored, or met with response), that response, in effect is a non-response. You will have to repeat the above question, loud enough for them, and others within ear distance, to hear, just as if you were a broken record. What the other party will realize is that you are not going to "ignore them" nor "challenge them." Instead, you are going to professionally "engage them."

Your engaging question communicates, without saying, "Put up or shut up." If the other party does offer a solid response that is fully comprehensible, don't attempt to assume its meaning. Simply turn to them and politely ask, "Could you please elaborate on that comment?"

Remember, as the leader, you are always in pursuit of the most viable solutions (as measured against three variables – ethics, legality, cost,) thoughts and action-plans, regardless their source. To calmly respond, when others would rather engage in storming behavior, is an expectation of a leader, especially in the storm of criticism.

Another strategic engagement to consider, when you know a thought that you are going to bring into action may cause a storm, is to flow smoothly and effectively to the next issue that may appeal to the largest number of stakeholders, thereby deflecting some of the attention from an otherwise stormy situation. This **"Continual Forward Momentum"** signals to others that you have moved beyond the otherwise stormy situation.

Weathering the storm of criticism is about your mindset and how you see others and your situation – ***attitude.*** With the right constructive attitude, the deployment of leader-driven behaviors to weather any storm of criticism is possible!

"Heroes are those who have changed history for the better. They are not always the men or women of highest potential, but those who have exploited their potential on society's behalf. Their deeds are not done for the honor, but for the duty. Through our study of heroes, we enter the realities of greatness."
- Fred Smith, Founder, FedEx

SECTION SIX:
Centering

Chapter 20	Centering Yourself and Staying Grounded
Chapter 21	Centering Others for Their Greatness Within
Chapter 22	Centering the Workplace Environment For Success: The Most Overlooked Ingredient

Chapter TWENTY
Centering Yourself and Staying Grounded: Finding Your Inner Mettle for Sustained Passion!

"He that does good to another does also good to himself; not only in the consequences, but in the act of doing it; for the consciousness of well-doing is an ample reward."
- Seneca

As the leader of an organization, it is essential to be a beacon from which others can seek guidance and direction. The leader's ability to be that beacon will come from how grounded and centered that individual is on the things that matter.

The annals of history consistently reveal that all leaders operate, more often than not, from three key answers. It is the sum of all three answers, which affords a leader his or her direction and allows them to stay grounded. This is what gives them the centeredness to which others gravitate!

They stay within three key areas that provide them with these three answers. And, when they have to step outside of these three key areas, they seek an individual, who they will not second-guess, who can answer these three key areas. This act of self-control is what makes them a "leader" … it is why people follow them.

I am reminded of these three key elements of leadership mettle, by observing my friend and CEO of the *Narrative Television Network*, Mr. Jim Stovall. He frames the **"Three Key Leader Answers,"** or sources of how stable and solid one's metal will be, by asking three questions:

1. **What do I know?** The answer will be based upon one's knowledge (technical and non-technical), education (formal and informal), personal experience (family, friends, community, social, health, spiritual, and inspirational), professional experience (jobs, employers, colleagues, customers, projects, assignments, travel, etc.), observations, and intuitiveness, and so on.

2. **How do I know this?** What truths do I know to be so, and exactly what is it that tells me this? What did I personally do or witness that tells me this conclusively?

3. **When did it dawn on me?** At what time in my life did I come to this realization? What are my stories and vignettes, or where was I when this became clear to me?

A leader's inner metal is derived from these three answers, and this becomes an eternal source of passion within them. Their passion becomes a never-ending source of motivation, and others look to this presence for even greater leadership.

These answers also serve to keep one grounded, by revealing the subjects, issues, and priorities to which a leader should (or should not) focus. By answering these three questions, one evolves to grounded leadership positions. In essence, you are defining your "Identity" (the "who" you really are) and "Purpose" (the "what" and "why" factors that evolve around your "Identity," and which you hold important).

Conversely, one becomes "off-centered" when one looses focus, strays from that which they know and can answer and are left to fake it.

When you find yourself mentally wandering aimlessly and lacking the youthful spring of energy, chances are extremely good that you have diverted from one of the key answer areas and are attempting to be all things to all people. Worse yet is finding yourself correcting and micromanaging others, who are capable of answering the three key leader questions in a specific area, when you, in fact, cannot.

Centering yourself and staying grounded starts by finding your inner mettle and holding on to it for sustained passion!

"When we see men of worth, we should think of becoming like them; when we see men of a contrary character, we should turn inward and examine ourselves."
- Confucius

Chapter TWENTY-ONE
Centering Others For Their
Greatness Within:
Helping Others to Find Their Inner
Mettle For Sustained Passion

"All the world's a stage, and all the men and women in it,
merely players. They have their exits and their entrances,
and one man in his time plays many parts."
- William Shakespeare

If a tree falls in a forest, and there is no one there to hear it fall, does it still make a noise?

A question that causes critical thought ... Equally thought-provoking is the question, "If there is no one to be lead or no one wanting to be lead, is there a need for a leader?"

In working to help others focus on success and find their inner mettle for sustained passion, a leader becomes like an orchestra director, engaging each member of the group from his or her own perspective and, on their own merits, cultivating from within them their true uniqueness and greatness.

By tapping into that key element, the leader takes a mix of individuals with complimenting talents and leads them to a collective success. In evaluating this act, the leader must determine of what each individual's true mettle is comprised, and then work to help them become centered on their area with the greatest strength!

There are four areas, which inspire greatness, to which a leader can assist others to focus. In *YIELD MANAGEMENT* (ISBN# 1-57444-206-6 / US $29.95), I presented the *"BETA Factor©"* as a result of a survey of 500 leaders within the Fortune 100, Government Agencies and Associations. This study revealed that, during the course of their career, they had witnessed four core ingredients that lead individuals from within the team to a position of respect and leadership on the team.

Consider how you can cultivate those around you to become centered by assisting in the growth of their:

1. *Brains* - What can we do to avail others through every opportunity to grow? How can we develop their intellectual capital and apply that knowledge to further the learning process?

2. *Energy* - What can be done to create environments conducive to high energy and remove the obstacles that zap energy? What do you do as a leader by way of assigning projects and opportunities that further feeds their energy levels?

3. *Talent* – That application of one's abilities that cause their uniqueness.

4. *Attitude* – What factors can be used to condition or recondition one toward having the most constructive, healthy and balanced mindset possible? One's self-talk reveals volumes about his or her attitude and the shaping forces behind it.

The old rulebook for managerial-leaders suggested that people should be told what to do, when to do it, how to do it, and where to do it, and it is never their business as to why to do it. This also suggested that there would be no *"BETA Factor©"* on this day or within this organization. In today's environment, centering someone implies building from their greatness and finding a complimenting way to do so, affording both an organizational and personal victory!

"We are what we repeatedly do. Excellence, then, is not an act but a habit."
- Aristotle

Chapter TWENTY-TWO
Centering the Workplace Environment For Success: The Most Overlooked Ingredient!

"In business, excellence of performance manifests itself, among other things, in the advancing of methods and processes; in the improvement of products, in more perfect organization, eliminating friction as well as waste; in bettering the condition of the working men (women), developing their faculties and promoting their happiness; and in the establishment of right relations with customers and with the community."
- Louis D. Brandeis

The single individual factor over which a person has sole control and which has direct influence over one's behavior and, thus, destiny in life ... the most overlooked ingredient to individual and organizational success today ... **ATTITUDE!**

More than 100 years ago, Harvard professor and to many, the father of modern psychology, William James, determined this to be so. Later, B.F. Skinner and Albert Ellis furthered the studies and found this still be true.

Yet many still resist this finding with all their vigor. Interesting enough, these tend to be the very individuals whose entire annual income doesn't equal that of what those who do grasp this factor pay in annual taxes!

"Hire for attitude and train for skill!" That has been the business growth model for more than two decades for Southwest Airlines, the only aviation company to consistently make a profit every year that it has been operational!

Southwest is the only aviation company to consistently rate among the top of all American air carriers. And in a year (2001-2002) when all airline companies have laid off thousands of employees and posted historical financial losses, Southwest has posted profits and hired thousands of new employees in the same industry.

> *The answer is exceedingly simple ...*
> *the "personality-character" or DNA of their leadership,*
> *from the top downward, is that*
> *ATTITUDE shows you the way to prosperity.*

As a leader, it is incumbent upon you (you are that DNA, which gives the degree of life others will model) to recognize this hidden, and most overlooked ingredient, and work to cultivate it within each individual. Even more importantly, work to create and foster a work environment that is most conducive for this to blossom.

If one looks closely, this same model can be seen being replicated throughout all industries for true and lasting success – this is not exclusive to Southwest Airlines. Alarmingly though, it is far more consistent for leaders and business owners to overlook this simple ingredient to success.

Attitude can be seen and measured in a number of ways and projected as a sort of group persona as well. Consider what these indicators reveal:

1. The tone of voice with which one communicates.

2. The direct and indirect body language.

3. The breathing patterns and exhales in one-on-one conversations, within groups and especially in meetings.

4. The dress code of an individual (not just casual dress days).

5. One's posture when they walk, stand, and, sit in the work place.

6. How one approaches even the most routine tasks in their functional domain of responsibility.

7. Individuals' actions (actions speak volumes over the spoken word alone) before the typical workday begins, during lunch, and the end of the day.

8. Whether an individual projects the same image, actions, views, and persona one-on-one as they do in large group situations.

A powerful benchmark technique, as you are pursuing or cultivating this hidden ingredient in leading an organization towards its "centeredness," is to ask yourself how you can replicate four core growth elements:

1. **Respect** for both one's self and those around you. How can you have respect for others? What can you do to such a point that you are actually 'happy' to be there and 'happy' to arrive daily?

2. **Help**. How aggressively can you become cross-trained and cross-educated to be able to assist any other individual in need of help? No more excuses, reinforced by old Unionist protectionist mindsets of "That is not my job!" beliefs. Again, this will link you directly back to the DNA at the uppermost levels of an organization, and that permeates the entire organization.

3. **Hire For Attitude, Train for Skill**. A solid Southwest Airlines characteristic, and one that I have repeatedly seen replicated across the nation by our clients, who each have consistently been at the top of their respective industries!

   This is directly linked to spontaneously 'happy' people in a workplace. If you hire ugly people with bad attitude baggage, you will invest the remainder of your life in attitude development trainings and incentive programs to change their attitudes – wow!

4. **Freedom**. Remember that organizational guidelines and rules serve as benchmarks for clueless employees. Explore how you can create a safe-free environment for people to flex guidelines when their knowledge indicates customer (internal and external applications) purpose attainment by doing so. Make the work place a relaxed and enjoyable place to contribute, and allow for profitability to flow freely.

Centering the workplace for success by tapping into the most overlooked ingredient to life and organizational success will enable the greatness within everyone to shine to such a daily level that the quality and quantity of production will astound the outside observer. It will be like other airlines that can only "excuse away" the greatness, which Southwest Airlines continually experiences.

SECTION SEVEN:
Conflict Management

Chapter 23   Conflict Management MAPs© to Success

Chapter 24   Conflict Management, the Four-Engagement Options and The L-Grid

Chapter 25   Conflict Management, the Anatomy Intervention Model

Chapter TWENTY-THREE
Conflict Management For Inspired Leadership: Understanding the MAPs© For Successful Behaviors In Business Today

"Most conflicts arise because of difference of viewpoint on the destination that the parties seek; letting go begins when the parties are willing to focus on the actual steps necessary for success, and not just the destination!"
- Dr. Jeffrey Magee, CMC

Organizational success can become easily derailed when conflicts and confrontations arise, whether between individuals, business units, or with customers. A leader's ability to engage vested parties to work toward acceptable solutions or bring parties to a fast tracked resolution is a hallmark of a *Legendary Leader*.

Typically, conflicts among people arise because of two core reasons:

1. The parties in conflict are just like one another.
2. The parties in conflict don't know one another.

This can be an interesting dynamic, especially if the parties in conflict have been associated with one another for a period of time. Imagine telling individuals, who have lived or worked with one another for an extended period of time that they are in conflict because they don't know one another. After they object, defer to the other option, citing the two must be in conflict because they are like one another. This in and of itself can give way to a whole new level of conflicts all together!

This cause could be dramatically reduced if management would merely allow for players, especially new players, an opportunity to meet and learn one another's likes and dislikes before being thrust into work situations with one another.

By encouraging players to invest in some "get-to-know time" with each other, you would be allowing time for employees to gain a greater awareness of one another's *MAPs©* (a.k.a. *Mental Action Plans©* that guide their actions).

Only by having some insight into others MAPs can you begin to gage what their triggers may be. And from this heightened awareness of one another's MAPs, strategic engagement techniques can be designed and implemented for greater productivity and fewer conflicts.

An interesting pattern among organizational psychologists and family therapists reveals some powerful similarities among people, when it comes to reasons for conflicts and confrontations. People tend to become absorbed in conflicts and confrontations for the same reasons. The three most common reasons are:

1. **_Differences of Opinion_**, with opinions being based on intangible, vague stuff, and gut instincts.

2. ***Differences of Interpretations***, with interpretations being based upon a tangible, facts, evidence, and education.

3. ***Blame for Past***, as in blame for past wrongdoings or misdoings.

To address the base line causes of conflicts and confrontations among most people, focus your energies where success can be attained.

To engage another person with whom you may be in conflict or where there may be the potential for conflict, you want to conversationally move engagements from number one and three above to number two. Conflicts that arise due to 'condition number two' can be addressed and resolved, whereas the other two can never be resolved – let them go!

When one is in perceived conflict with others because of *"Differences of Interpretation,"* it is necessary to have all parties share with one another what their particular tangible facts, evidence, education, experiences, or substances are that have lead them to their particular "Interpretation."

It is at this point in the dialogue that it will become very evident from where the differences stem and thus, where the dialogue needs to focus – issue and substance oriented, not personality differences.

Once revealed and addressed, the conflict is typically very easily resolved. From here everyone can once again focus their energies on forward momentum and greater success!

Chapter TWENTY-FOUR
Conflict Management:
Leader or Loser?
Using The "L-Grid" to Identify Which of Four Intervention Strategies to Use For Resolution!

"Because some people just live to be bitter, ugly and negative, the reality of managing away many difficult situations and confrontational people is to select from one of four basic interaction options and recognize when doing nothing may be your most explosive intervention action plan of all!"
- Dr. Jeffrey Magee, CMC

There are two extreme behavioral patterns that one can experience when engaging another person, who is destined for a conflict or all-out confrontation. You can select an action plan that will allow you to shine as a "leader," or you can barge straight onward and increase the odds of ending as a "loser!"

To work through conflicts and confrontations and determine a logic-based, response driven *best-course-of-action (BCOA©)* every time, consider a lesson learned from today's Generation "X." The Gen Xer's have made famous the sign of raising one's left hand in an upward direction, with the index finger pointing upward and the thumb pointing outward in the fashion of a large letter "L." This sign is their universal language to represent "loser."

In management, this same symbol could be interpreted as an "L-grid." By visualizing this "L-grid," or in some instances, even graphing this out on a sheet of paper to plot multiple players or situations, you, as a manager or leader, will gain the ability to instantly lead one's own behavior away from that of "loser" and toward that of continuous "leader." This new instrument, born out of the "L-grid," becomes one's **"Action Engagement Model©."** By plotting a variable from low to high on the vertical axis and the same on the horizontal axis, one will be powerfully directed to their best course of action (BCOA©).

The Methodology of the "Action Engagement Model©" For Resolution: To measure and determine how best to engage, resolve, solve, manage, eliminate, avoid, or cope with negative, difficult, and confrontational situations or people, consider how you would measure the situation or person on the "L-grid." The vertical axis represents how you would score the level of "Reality Control" of a given variable, and the horizontal axis represents the level of "Impact for Better/Change" variables. Now, within this "L-grid," visualize both the vertical and horizontal axes, as if they were numbered one through 10. One through five represent unacceptable or negative scores, and six through 10 represent acceptable or positive scores. You can now score individuals and situations against this model.

If you really desire to address conflicts and confrontations for resolution, determine in which quadrant you would land the next time you felt compelled to engage either a person or situation. Within the "**Action Engagement Model L-grid©**" model, there are four basic quadrants from which you can guide your best-course-of-action (BCOA©) plans.

<u>*The Best-Course-Of-Action from the* "**Action Engagement**</u>
<u>**Model L-grid©**</u>": To determine exactly what to do, decide
whether you have or do not have "Control" over the person
or situation on the vertical axis line (low on the axis line
means "no," and high on the axis line means "yes"). After
that measurement determination, determine, on the
horizontal axis, if that person or situation were addressed,
would it really matter in respect to positive "Impact" or
constructive healthy change (low on the axis line means
"no," and high on the axis line means "yes"). Your course
of action in fast tracking how best to address conflicts and
confrontations:

1. Bottom left quadrant placement reveals that your
    BCOA is to "SHUT UP" and walk away. This
    quadrant represents items of no control and no
    impact; therefore, don't invest your time and
    energy.

2. Top left quadrant placement reveals that your
    BCOA is to "DROP IT" and leave the issue alone,
    as no one but you cares – it does not matter.

3. Bottom right quadrant placement reveals that, while
    "it" matters, you have no "control over it," so your
    BCOA is to determine who does have "Influence
    and Control" over "it," and work to "Influence"
    them to address the "it."

4. Top right quadrant placement is for those people
    and situations that should be on your "To do list."
    You have "Control," and the "Impact" would be
    worth the engagement.

Based upon whichever quadrant you find yourself, this **"Action Engagement Model©"** will direct you to design immediate action-plans. *ENOUGH ALREADY: 50 FAST Ways To Deal With, Manage and Eliminate Negativity At Work and Home* (ISBN# 0-9641240-9-2 / $12.95) details fifty such immediate action behaviors, designed to bring about positive and healthy outcomes.

To look back at the last series of conflicts and confrontations by which one has been consumed at home and in business and recognize the percentage of time invested in them as they relate to the four quadrants of the **"Action Engagement Model©"** may be alarming. Time spent on bottom left and top left quadrants are a percentage of time lost.

As a leader, one must maintain control, in potential conflict and confrontationally volatile times, and gage all actions in a manner that one may find him or herself on the right side quadrants. This is the best investment of a leader's time!

Chapter TWENTY-FIVE

Conflict Management: Using the "Anatomy-of-a-Conflict" Model to Work Through Major Conflicts and Confrontations For Resolution! Learn How to "Let Go" Once And For All ...

"When passions and emotions are electrified, resolving a conflict is practically impossible ... to find a logical means of engaging the parties and focusing energies away from that which perpetuates negativity and increased conflict and toward resolution is a critical must. Look for a template for success at this point!"
Dr. Jeff Magee, PDM, CSP, CMC

Today's management and leadership giants like Drucker, Morrisey, and Senge talk of the high percentage of business and technological advances, which have occurred in the past century as a result of conflicts and change-necessitated issues. Businesses have invested more training dollars into conflict resolution training in the past decade than any other soft-skill training topic.

Sometimes, no matter what you do, becoming engulfed in a conflict and confrontation with others is going to be a business reality. It is in these emotionally electrified environments that a controlled and systematic approach to conflict management and, thus, resolution is necessary.

In most cases, presenting doctrine on how to address and resolve these apex level conflicts just doesn't work. Validate that fact!

> *Have you ever experienced a past conflict,*
> *thought to be resolved, that raises its ugly head and*
> *comes back in a new conflict? If so, then you only*
> *addressed the surface issues in that historical matter.*
> *And the reason is due, in large part, to the fact that if you*
> *engage another party in conflict resolution, you must be*
> *able to reveal and address all of the conflict anatomy.*

Compounding conflicts is due to many individuals' inability to get beyond the surface and effectively and non-combatively deal with the real substance of a conflict for final resolution. *To effectively deal with an involved conflict and "bury the proverbial hatchet," focus your efforts on three steps detailed in the "Anatomy-of-a-Conflict©" model.*

Here is a powerful matrix that will aid you in facilitating a dialogue with others. This model (a.k.a. the Anatomy Of A Conflict© Model) assists to ensure that all parties' interests are revealed and addressed, if in fact the aim is to reach an acceptable final resolution by all parties.

STEP ONE – Basic Information Identification: Visualize or, when appropriate, draw a large "plus sign" on a piece of paper, white board, flip chart, etc. This "plus sign" matrix creates four quadrants that will guide the conversation to determine the core data necessary from each quadrant and aid to avoid the temptation to defend or challenge any specific quadrant. "Step One" is to get the basic information out in the open.

1. Let the vertical axis represent the difference between the left side, representing "you" and your needs, and the right side, representing "them" and their needs.

2. Let the horizontal line represent the difference between "Position Statements" (the "what factor" one wants or needs) above the line and "Interest Statements" (the "why," also seen as one's motivators – what they have initially identified as needing) below the line.

With this "plus sign" model, visualize the top left quadrant as quadrant one, top right quadrant as quadrant two, bottom left as quadrant three, and bottom right as quadrant four. Thus quadrants one and three deal with "you" and quadrants two and four deal with the "other party."

At any point in this due diligence dialogue, if there is a quadrant that is unknown or unclear to you as the facilitator to conflict resolution, then that is the quadrant toward which the attention needs to be directed.

STEP TWO – Scale Of Flexibility: As you listen to the information revealed from "Step One" (quadrants one through four), listen for what each party initially pre-ports to be seeking. Then work to see what other levels of acceptable resolutions there may be, without asking either party to make concessions. This range of acceptable resolutions is their "Scale Of Flexibility©."

An example: If you had to fly from one city to another, arrived at the airport in time for the last flight out and were told that there was only one seat remaining, would that meet your minimum need level? If that seat were a middle seat in the last row, would it still meet that need? On your "Scale Of Flexibility" there would be a wide range of other, and gradually better, acceptable resolution answers!

STEP THREE – Common Ground: As an outgrowth of all of the information that surfaces through Step One and Step Two of the "**Anatomy-of-a-Conflict©**" model, some sort of "Common Ground" between the two sides can be attained.

This is where you begin to reach a lasting and sustained resolution. By identifying the "Common Ground" among the parties involved, the sides can now move away from their obvious differences, back in "Step One," when everyone was initially only focused on their own "Position Statements," and concentrate on similarities. From here, resolution is within reach; as a leader, you can aim everyone's energies toward shared success.

As a leader, one's ability to facilitate healthy dialogue in the height of conflicts and aim interpersonal energies in the direction of fact-based, issue dialogue, and not personal attacks, is critical.

Leaders today will face potential conflict and confrontation situations as a norm, given the ever growing, diverse generational segmentations, cultural differences, and passion that individuals bring to the work place. It is resolution through viable action plans that leads to greater productivity and profitability, which all leaders must attain to be viable both today and tomorrow!

SECTION EIGHT:
Life Balance

Chapter 26   Life Balance as a Leader:
               From 97 Percent to 3 Percent
Chapter 27   Life Balance as a Leader: Life
               Cycle Direction
Chapter 28   Life Balance as a Leader: Time
               to Leave

Chapter TWENTY-SIX
100 Percent Life Balance as a Leader: Moving From the Dominant 97 Percent, to the Select 3 Percent "X" Club

"There is a significant difference between being active and being productive ... the truly successful know this, concentrate on this and allow themselves to only be productive in all that they do and with all whom they associate!"
- Jim Stovall, CEO, Emmy Award Winning, Narrative Television Network

It is fascinating to observe that, whenever anyone or any organization notes the percentage of an index recognized as most accomplished, most celebrated, or most earned, that percentage seems to range between three to five percent of any population index.

For example: "X-percentage" of high school athletes receive college scholarships; "X-percentage" of college athletes will make it professionally; members of MENSA make up "X-percentage" of the population; the disproportionate amount of Federal income tax is paid by "X-percentage" of the population; a tax break would disproportionately benefit "X-percentage" of a population; and so on and so on.

142 Building a Legendary Leader

In a society where people are continuously bombarded with negative stimulants (office politics, government leaders who have never been in business to understand what it takes to generate capital, mainstream mass media, road rage, discourteous neighbors, etc.) and it has become fashionable for litigious actions to become common place, people look for any number of excuses for their station in life. Compounding this out-of-balance life of leaders and managers are individuals, who deflect attention from their own accountability and prefer to blame others for their lot in life (which may be generationally and culturally influenced and induced).

For these types of reasons, the spotlight truly does fall on a small percentage of those that have chosen to excel instead of derail – **"The Select 3 Percent!"**

3 percent of any population index have chosen "success" as their journey in life, while 97 percent have chosen to "suc(cess)!"

To maintain a life balance as a leader today, one must maintain an inner mental balance and forward moving dialogue with oneself. This is especially important in the presence of those who would rather go in a 97-Percent direction.

Napoleon Hill and W. Clement Stone, in their classic book, *Success Through A Positive Mental Attitude* (ISBN# 0-671-82661-1), offered a label for this powerfully positive inner mental balance into which one could tap in order to maintain forward momentum. Their assertion was that the successful few maintain within them an active *"Mental Board Of Directors"* – a concept that even the 97-Percenters maintain. The difference is that the 97-

Percenters choose to populate it with negative influences, influencers, and individuals!

In my publication and audio, *POWER CHARGED FOR LIFE®* (ISBN# 0-9641240-4-1), the concept of a *"Mental Board Of Directors"* is further developed. To maintain one's life balance personally and professionally, realize that a simplified way to gain a better understanding of one's mindset in the most normal of circumstances is to recognize that, before any behavioral pattern is exhibited, one has an instantaneous *"Inner Voice Dialogue©"* with oneself.

This inner dialogue is lead by any one or combination of five different core sets of occupants in one's *"Board."* To ensure, as a leader, you posses positive inner dialogue and are a member of this 3-Percent, participate in the following exercise:

1. Flex open one of your hands and reflect upon your five fingers. In your head, pull up those people, past or present, which occupy your mental space. These would be the various individuals that you may occasionally mentally reflect on for guidance, advice, counsel, or suggestions. In essence, identify those names that would be on your mental roster.

2. Now, as you pull up this mental roster or inventory of individuals, attribute one name per finger and fold that finger down. As you continue this drill, recognize the number of individuals that immediately come to you. These are the members of your *"Mental Board Of Directors."*

3. As you drill down the names in your head that occupy this unique space, you may recognize that there are some names that you have consciously placed into this position and some that have worked their way onto your *"Board"* that should be terminated immediately (as they may be 97-Percenters). Most people also recognize that their hand is transformed from an open hand to a fist position with the drill down, and most people immediately recognize about five members.

4. I refer to this *"Mental Board Of Directors"* concept as one's *"FIST Factor©."* This is where one gets and, thereby, can cultivate greater *"Inner Voice Dialogue"* for sustained and increased 3-Percent Club membership!

To develop life balance and excel as a leader, one must realize that how one is conditioned to think (logic and rationalization abilities) and feel (emotion and gut instinct abilities), directly influences how one will interact and lead others today and tomorrow. If one likes what that reveals, then a leader would desire to continue to subject themselves to similar stimulants and people. Conversely, if your inner leader and objective *"Inner Voice Dialogue"* were to reveal to you a need to recondition some of how you think and feel in order to be more effective, then you must start with your *FIST Factor©*. As you take your clinched fist and shake it, you realize that it is your *FIST Factor©* from which you draw your power, strength, and energy.

A well-balanced *FIST Factor©* (*"Mental Board Of Directors"*) should contain five types of members (your *"Board"* may consist of fewer or greater numbers of members, with some occupying more than one position on your "*Board*"). Cross reference the following **FIST Factor©** positions and recognize that if any position is vacant, it is time to go on a mental job search mission. Here are the five members to a powerfully positive **FIST Factor©**:

1. **Family** – Look at your immediate and extended family tree. Most people have multiple personality types, and your family knows a specific family side of you for which this member will hold you accountable.

2. **Friend** – Most people have a personality type that only their friends see and know; therefore, this member will hold this other side of you accountable.

3. **Profession** – Someone in the universe who shares your profession should be on your "*Board/FIST Factor.*" When you need professional advice, you will have someone who can help. Family and friends are familiar with you; therefore, they can't be professionally objective.

4. **Underdog** – This would be that person that you know, who faces adversity and challenges. However, instead of digressing into that 97-Percent Club, this person demonstrates resiliency and bounces back with vigor and dignity, ultimately succeeding.

5. **Success** – The single-most successful person you know personally should also be on your "*Board/FIST Factor.*" By personal observation and

interaction, you can learn to replicate their models of behavioral success. You will have a person to mentally reference or physically engage before taking action.

Each of these people serves to provide you with mental maps to greatness, success, and life balance insight. The only way to ensure that you will be in that 3-Percent is to ensure that your *FIST Factor©* members are, themselves, 3-Percenters – not 97-Percenters!

The most devastating factor to personal life balance and leader success is if your *FIST Factor©* is made up of 97-Percenters, as you will be more inclined to listen to and follow their advise, versus that of the 3-Percenters.

To ensure that you maintain that 3-Percent edge, always push yourself to add to your intellectual net worth (go to www.KeepingTheEdge.com). And ensure that you enrich how you think, talk, and act as a leader by enlarging your *FIST Factor©* with only 3-Percenters!

> *"Whether you think you can or think you can't,*
> *you are correct!"*
> *Henry Ford*

Chapter TWENTY-SEVEN
Life Balance as a Leader:
Nine Phases Of One's "Life Cycle" ...
What Counts and What Doesn't

"Success is more so in the journey than it is in the destination. Life balance is about the care in the steps and the nine phases of one's life, more so than in where one ends."
- Dr. Jeff Magee, CSP, CMC

As a leader, keeping balance in one's life is critical for sustained performance. To serve as a model of performance excellence and a beacon to which others can look for guidance, commitment, and energy, leaders must have a greater understanding of what maintains their own balance and how to give similar direction to the teams with whom they associate and lead.

Most leaders reach a critical point of either "flaming out" or allowing their efforts to cause them to "derail" an otherwise potentially great career, due to inadequate balance in life cycle. Medical science would assert that individuals have nine zones of life energy – nine zones from which one can set goals and priorities, nine zones within which one lives daily. If any one of the nine zones is unconsciously neglected, one can become out of balance.

When any one zone becomes so neglected that it is not cared for, one becomes susceptible to life derailment. For most people, an out-of-balance existence is only realized when one is faced with a catastrophic trauma. Most common trauma points are:

1. Financial – when one loses a job or realizes they cannot meet their obligations.

2. Health – when one has neglected this to a point that normal function is impaired, or one ends up in a hospital seeking medical care for life maintenance needs.

There are, however, nine zones that constitute one's "Life Cycle." From this "Life Cycle" concept, one's life can be managed to maintain balance or neglected until one finds oneself so out of balance that trauma is the inevitable destination. Then, as a leader, their functionality is jeopardized, and everyone around them becomes penalized.

Consider the following nine "Life Cycle" phases as categories of a pie chart, with each wedge appropriately labeled. Then score yourself against them to determine your balance.

1. **Professional** - employment issues that land one on an unemployment list.

2. **Family** – personal issues that precipitate family breakups, divorce, adolescent rebellion, closeness with others, etc.

3. **Community** – involvement and standing among those around you; how one perceives they are being served.

4. **Financial** – how secure one feels economically; the earning capacity one maintains.

5. **Inspirational** – how one feels supported and nurtured to and from others.

6. **Social** – the interactions among others; outlets one can access.

7. **Health** – how one feels about his or her overall physical stature and performance.

8. **Education** – the level of intellectual capacity one has, develops, and maintains, which influences one's future.

9. **Spiritual** – the sense of purpose and belonging one maintains.

As a leader in one's personal and professional life, balance brings about greater performance ability and feeds one's passion. That, in turn, builds increased motivation. Consider how you, as a leader, would score these nine phases or zones, as visualized within a pie chart. There are two critical questions to measure on a scale of zero (low) to 10 (high):

1. ***How well do I feel I perform that life zone?*** This becomes a very powerful question in recognizing (again, self-perception) how you score each independent zone from the other, and, when you are done, how that zone connects to the others in the pie chart. In essence, after you have recognized the score for each zone or pie chart wedge, do they appear relatively smooth around the perimeter or is

there a definite disparity among some of the wedges? Now, before you begin evaluating whether you are doing good (in balance) or bad (out of balance), consider question two!

2. ***How important is it to me?*** The score from question one must be placed into perspective with how important you feel that zone or pie chart wedge is in your life at any given time. If someone else prescribes any particular zone as important, but you scored it low in question one, you would be placing unfair stress upon yourself to perform. However, if you score low in a category in both question one and two, the low score does not really matter!

Therefore, question two is the most important to maintaining Life Balance. The "Life-Cycle" exercise reveals those phases or zones that are "most important"; those are the zones with which one should work in order to ensure that there is a high score of "performance" as well.

Leaders that perform at peak performance, and can sustain that level of performance and standard for others, have balance. Maintaining that balance is critical for leadership development, leadership modeling, and derailment avoidance. Are you in balance?

Chapter TWENTY-EIGHT
Life Balance as a Leader:
Knowing When it is Time to Leave

"You've got to know when to hold them, and you've got to know when to fold them ..."
- Kenny Rogers

Maintaining life balance is an obligation of a leader to both themselves and those they serve. Knowing when one is out of balance, at the detriment of the organization one serves, is a powerful clue that it is time to leave.

Human resource professionals and executive leadership placement firms continue to report that the leading indicators of leader employment departures have less to do with financial reasons and more to do with general performance issues. In fact, a 2002 study by Robert Half International reveals that individuals most often leave due to:

1. Limited opportunities and advancement.

2. Lack of acknowledgement, appreciation, and recognition.

3. Boredom with position and lack of meaningful challenge.

4. Inadequate benefits and salary.

As a leader, it is important to maintain life balance by feeding it with meaningful experiences and contributions, both professionally and personally. Contributing to an entity and receiving something back is essential for a leader to maintain balance. When either ceases, a leader begins to become complacent and robotic in his or her actions, leaving the momentum of the organization and others, prior to this break point, as the only contributing factors to success. Once that break point occurs, the leader has outlived his or usefulness!

Here are some indicators that it is time to leave and regain life balance:

1. The passion for what one does has to be artificially induced.

2. You no longer find yourself eager to wake in the morning and tackle what you do professionally.

3. You find yourself no longer concerned with the development of others within a business for the sake of a continued prosperous, profitable tomorrow.

4. You no longer daydream of professional advancements, innovations, new endeavors, etc.

5. You have to be motivated by others to participate and contribute as a norm. People fail to gravitate towards you, as the natural leader and energy source, for a sense of belonging and purpose.

6. You no longer genuinely feel as if you have skill, knowledge, and practical growth experience to offer to others and the organization. Your mental

faculties have shut down operation, and you feel a natural resistance toward learning and experience-building opportunities.

7. You find more comfort, and even recreation, in complaining and finding fault with others and other things than being a source of solution and expansion.

8. You find that your dominating thoughts and objectives revolve around how you can secure greater riches for yourself.

The vast richness and reserves of intellectual capital within organizations across the globe on a daily basis is overwhelming. A leader with some degree of balance within his or her personal and professional life has the ability to tap into those riches. Better yet, a leader with a degree of balance has the innate ability to tap into his or her intellectual bank account and make appropriate deposits with others for their gain.

As a leader, if you fail to recognize, or even desire to recognize, the opportunities, it is time to leave. Far too often, instead of making this exit while at the top of their game and the organization's apex, leaders linger on. Then, what gains and legitimate contributions they have made become overshadowed by the descending negative reputation that hangs around their neck.

It is easy to know when to leave if you are out of balance and there is no desire to regain that balance while in your present station.

SECTION NINE:
Leadership Engagement

Chapter 29	Leadership Engagement: Six Intervention Styles
Chapter 30	Leadership Engagement: Instant Identification and Succession Planning Made Easy
Chapter 31	Leadership Engagement: "Span-Of-Control" Drives Empowerment
Chapter 32	Leadership Engagement: The Five W's and One H of Intervention

Chapter TWENTY-NINE
Leadership Engagement:
Six Leadership-Coaching Intervention Styles Can Ensure You Don't Fall Into the Micro-Management Trap

"I would rather excel in the knowledge of what is excellent, than in the extent of my power."
- Alexander the Great

As a leader within an organization, your capacity to know when and how best to engage another person is critical to avoiding the micro-management trap. The micro-management trap is doing the wrong thing at the right time, and it can frustrate a potentially great member of the team!

Further compounding the frustrations and downside of miss-cued interventions is the loss in productivity that occurs from management reading an engagement situation incorrectly or an employee who becomes further de-motivated.

There are six applicable management, leadership, or coaching (whatever label you wish to place on your reason for engaging another person) intervention styles that can be deployed, depending upon a situation and the player or employee involved (For more information and ideas, get your copy of *COACHING for IMPACT: The Art & Leadership Of Generational Coaching®*, Brown Books, ISBN# 0-9641240-3-3 /USA $29.95).

To best visualize each intervention style, consider them as engagement "hats" on a hat rack. Each hat has a name, and each hat serves a very specific purpose. Having a better understanding of the purpose, intent, and responsibility of each will direct you as to when to reach for any one particular hat, and when to leave the others on the hat rack. Wearing the incorrect hat at any given time is a simple definition of micro-management.

The six managerial-leadership-coaching engagement styles are:

1. *Manager* – This is a hands-on function that requires you to stop your other actions and focus solely on that person for best effect. Here, intent is to educate or train an individual on that which they don't know, but must understand in order to be functional. Sometimes it is necessary to ensure others understand rules, policies, and procedures, as well, in order to function properly.

2. *Teacher* – All of the exact intervention actions, as detailed in the "manager" style, apply here as well. The primary difference between this style and that of the "manager" is that a "teacher" must also be very patient. This poses a potential problem for a manager, who is unwilling to slow down to engage. One also must posses the basic functional knowledge of that which they are compelled to impart to another. This intervention act can be sabotaged if the "teacher" does not posses a working understanding knowledge; this happens every day in organizations – the brain-dead teaching the unknown!

3. ***Counselor*** – This is a hands-on function that requires you to stop your other actions and focus solely on that person for best effect. Here, the goal is to engage a person with a behavioral pattern that, through other engagement styles, has not produced a desired change. Their actions now have risen to the level of being a serious problem that no longer can be ignored.

   Here, your best course of action could be to ask yourself if this action requires other participants to address it. If not, proceed by meeting one-on-one in private. Address the severity of the problem and maintain issue orientation. Have an agenda. Detail the potential pain factors that they can undergo if a before arriving to a change. Acknowledge your desire to work with them, keep them, and develop a mutual action solution plan. Set a follow-up date to get back together; monitor progress and decide to what degree you want to document (or not) these interactions. Remember, your intent here is to resolve the team's (and your) headache; it is not Dale Carnegie time. Don't attempt to win friends and influence people here; this is your time, not theirs!

4. ***Disciplinarian*** – This includes all of the exact actions detailed in the "counselor" intervention hat, as well as an understanding that you will never have the same engagement on this matter again. Document all of your actions and detail how any further continued action would constitute grounds for immediate dismissal. Better yet, have a document, acknowledging this fact, prepared for them to sign!

5. ***Mentor*** - This is a hands-on function that requires you to stop your other actions and focus solely on that person for best effect. Here, intent here is to avail oneself to the other person (and in some organizations that would be an assigned individual, ideally two operational levels removed from you). You want to serve as an advisor and display an appropriate willingness to encourage them from both the sidelines and interactively.

6. ***Coach*** - This is a hands-off function that does not require you to actively engage the other person, participating with them on their level and on what they are accountable for. The "coach" is primarily responsible for motivating the individual. A greater understanding of each individual player on your team will afford you a greater understanding of what each individual's motivating triggers are. Here, you serve as a nurturer and encourager to ensure the individual maintains a positive attitude and you continually work to create an environment conducive for all players to exhibit a winning attitude. Studies have found that one's attitude directly influences one's actions; conversely, one's actions further reinforce one's attitude!

While management may have positive intent, wearing the wrong hat at any given time merely creates an opportunity for the derailment of both management and employees.

Only one of the six possible leadership intervention styles is "hands-off," while the others require a "hands-on" approach. For that reason, micro-management is a trap into which it is easy to fall!

You can now avoid micro-management with style and flair in your next intervention purpose. Whether it be one-on-one or within group situations, consider what you are reaching for and demonstrate the best leadership engagement style for what your needs are at any given time!

Chapter THIRTY
Leadership Engagement: Instant Identification and Succession Planning Made Easy For Proper Use of the Six Leadership-Coaching Intervention Styles

Using the Leadership-Coaching "SA Engagement Model" to Plot Your Best Course of Actions Can Ensure a Winning Team.

"Nothing is perfect from every point of view."
- Horace

As a leader, one must be able to, in an instance, notice one's mental and physical abilities in order to direct their actions for immediate positive and lasting effect.

One trap that many managers, leaders, and business coaches fall victim to is the mentality that once one ascends into that realm of leadership, they must be compelled to have all of the solutions and answers. This is a fast track to stress, anxiety, and the derailment of one's career. It is better to approach leadership from the perspective of how one needs to engage those around them in order to generate responses and solutions to critical questions, asked at the right time.

Management may be one of the easiest positions to which one can ascend ...

*if one would retrain themselves to not feel compelled
to have the answers, but rather learn how to ask
rapid fire, sequential questions at the right time,
stimulating ideas and viable solutions from themselves
and those around them!*

Depending upon a situation and the player or employee involved, there are six applicable management, leadership, or coaching (whatever label you wish to place on your reason for engaging another person) intervention styles that can be deployed.

To best visualize which intervention style would yield the greatest net result, in your next email exchange, telephone dialogue, one-on-one intervention, or group engagement, consider the following model as a template that can guide your actions to greater productive outcomes.

Take your left hand and place it out in front of you, with your index finger pointing vertically upwards and your thumb horizontally outward. While Generation "X'ers" would say this image creates the letter "L" for loser, the leader within you can also see this gesture creates a "L-grid." As you move to engage another person, use this "L-grid" mentally actually plot it out on a sheet of paper. By measuring two variables on the axis lines, you will be directed to the best leadership intervention style suitable for deployment.

The methodology of this *'SA Engagement Model©''* is to measure Skill and Attitude:

1. **Vertical Axis** – From low (bottommost placements) to high (uppermost placements), you simply measure "Skill/Knowledge" on this scale. You

would measure the perceived or known level of skill or knowledge of the other party that you need to engage on this scale. You could affix ascending numbers to both axis lines, with a score of 'five' serving as the breaking point between acceptable and unacceptable.

2. **Horizontal Axis** – From low (left placement) to high (right placement), you simply measure "Attitude" on this scale. You would measure the perceived or known level of attitude of the other party in need of intervention on this scale.

3. Plot the two lines and connect them accordingly. This will place you into one of the four primary quadrants that the "L-grid" creates. Within the lower left and lower right quadrants you can impose an additional quadrant in the lower left most portion of each of those, thus creating a total of six quadrants. Each quadrant is labeled with a leadership intervention style, which will direct you as to how best to intervene with the other person.

The power of this *"SA Engagement Model©"* is that it affords a leader two different action plans:

1. It can be used <u>as a "Specific Incident Guide,"</u> enabling a manager, leader, or coach to engage anyone at any time and deploy the best engagement style.

2. Also, it can be used <u>as a "Succession Planning Guide,"</u> measuring all of one's direct reports from an overall perspective on each axis line. This will determine where every individual player scores and

lands. It then will drive the developmental intervention plans necessary for leaders to be able to grow each player accordingly, ensure that an organization can survive and determine who comprises their actual future talent pool!

So, where one lands on the scale would dictate what the appropriate intervention style would be. You can defer to the previous chapter for detailed traits and characteristics of each of the following leadership engagement styles (For more information and ideas get your copy of *YIELD MANAGEMENT: The Leadership Alternative for Performance and Net Profit Improvement*, by CRC Press, ISBN# 1-57444-206-6 /USA $29.95). The answers are:

1. **Coach** – The top left quadrant reveals a player with high skill and low attitude; pursue attitude issues.

2. **Counselor** – The bottom left quadrant reveals a player with low skill and low attitude – you must address each.

3. **Disciplinarian** – The bottommost left quadrant reveals a person with no functional knowledge or skill on needed matters and a highly combative attitude.

4. **Manager** – The bottom right quadrant reveals a person with little to low skill and an otherwise healthy attitude. Engage and give them the necessary functional skills to proceed.

5. **Teacher** – The bottommost right quadrant reveals a person who has no skill or knowledge of how to proceed, yet is happy about it. Cease the

opportunity to grow and nurture quickly, before they become frustrated and their attitude slides downhill.

6. **Mentor** – The top right quadrant is where you find people that posses the skill and knowledge to be productive and have a winning attitude. Merely make yourself available to these winners so, when they need or desire intervention, they can seek you and others out. Don't derail their desire for forward momentum!

You can greatly enhance your leadership engagement abilities by using this "SA Engagement Model©." It will allow you to instantly identify the player in a more objective manner. As a leader, you can also improve your overall succession planning by plotting all of your direct reports onto this model. It will, in turn, dictate the deployment of the most appropriate of the six leadership-coaching intervention styles for each player as you ultimately work to evolve all players into the "Mentor" quadrant!

Using the "SA Engagement Model©" to plot your best course of action can ensure a winning team, now and into the future!

Chapter THIRTY-ONE
Leadership Engagement:
The "Span-of-Control©" One
Undertakes Dictates The Level Of
Empowerment Others Assume!

"He who will not apply new remedies must expect new evils, for time is the greatest innovator."
- Francis Bacon

As a leader, the level of commitment and dedication that those around them assume is in direct proportion to the degree of control, authority, and responsibility the leader assumes or constructively abdicates at any given time. Conversely, this has a direct influence on the overall growth and development or stagnation and decline of individuals and, ultimately, an organization.

By reflecting on how one tends to approach management from a broad perspective and how organizations approach the management of resources and personnel assets, effective leadership engagements can be crafted for the well being of all concerned. Consider the *"Span-of-Control©"* leadership model to be a template from which actions can be guided toward greater levels of empowerment of individuals and teams.

Mentally visualize, or draw on a sheet of paper, an L-grid with a diagonal line from the bwer left hand corner of the grid to the upper right hand corner. Now, label the vertical axis with "Control/Authority" from low levels (bottom measurements) to high levels (upward measurements). Label the horizontal axis with "Time/Complexity," again from low levels (leftmost measurements) to high levels (rightmost measurements).

Determining the level of control that is the tendency of any individual manager or leader is simple using this template. Make a dissection mark on the diagonal line, indicating at what level, from lower left to upper right placement, best represents the comfort zone tendency based upon the level of control or authority a leader tends to seek or demonstrate.

How close to the left the dissection mark is indicates:

1. A greater propensity for autocratic management style.

2. Less tolerance for individual creativity or deviation from the normal performance behavior, expected or prescribed as acceptable.

3. More likelihood of bureaucracy to develop and be perpetuated.

4. Less likely to experience high levels of buy-in, commitment, creativity, and dedication from individuals.

5. Loyalty of individuals to both the organization and the leader become very transparent or nonexistent.

As a leader, you can quickly realize that, in order to move your managerial-leadership style rightward on the diagonal line, you must continually look for "Opportunities" to let go, grow, and develop those around you. Empowerment begins only at the halfway point on the diagonal line. As you find yourself as the leader toward the right, your *"Span-of-Control©"* will begin to decline, and that of the other person will greatly increase. While this may be initially uncomfortable to you, you leadership quotient will ultimately grow and benefit both you and the other person.

Sometimes there may be many reasons that relinquishing control to others may be difficult:

1. Generational segmentation of the other person.

2. Obstacles of cultural diversity and differences.

3. Complexity of the issue needing to be addressed.

4. Crisis mode may warrant greater control on behalf of the leader, and, if not clearly communicated as the "why" factor, will impact the performance of others.

5. Experience levels of all parties involved. This, in itself, reveals a need to further develop the other person.

6. Low expectations or self-esteem of the leaders themselves.

Human nature is that individuals become more energized, committed, dedicated, creative, and willing to work on those things with which greater "Control/Authority" is experienced. (See www.KeysToMySuccess.com for more.)

Sometimes, in order to attain a higher level of productivity and proficiency from your team, you may need to serve as a "shock absorber" between the organization's ***"Span-of-Control©"*** personality, as measured on the model (if it scores a leftmost placement on the diagonal line), and what you may need to demonstrate (a further right personal placement on the diagonal line) in order to gain peak performance from those you lead.

Chapter THIRTY-TWO
Leadership Engagement:
The Five W's and One H of
Successful Intervention!

"To appear to be on the inside and know more than others
about what is going on is a great temptation for most
people. It is a rare person who is willing to seem
to know less than he does."
- Eleanor Roosevelt

A lesson from the halls of high school English can directly apply to effective leadership intervention in the hallways of business.

As a simple template, imagine having six basic letters emblazoned on the inside of one's eyelids to guide every managerial-leadership engagement with others. Immediately before initiating any action, you could quickly scan each letter and determine if you are prepared to address that specific letter in the manner and depth appropriate for the individual or group with which you are about to interact.

As management consultant, working with the Fortune 100 leading associations, it is practically guaranteed that when there is organizational dysfunction, it is typically due to one of the six critical management letters being missed.

Imagine the number one letter to human motivation as the *"Bridge to Why."* Managers and leaders sabotage their best intentions by drafting great prose, addressing the "What" and "How" of yesterday's actions and the new "What" and "How" of today and tomorrow's (*YIELD MANAGEMENT: The Leadership Alternative for Performance and Net Profit Improvement*, by CRC Press, ISBN# 1-57444-206-6 /USA $29.95). However, they completely overlook the importance of connecting those two sides with reasoned explanation to the "Why" factor - the *"Bridge to Why."*

Most managers have a thorough grasp of the functionality letters and often miss the perspective letters of management and leadership. A manager is capable of barking out:

1. **What** – factors of a policy, procedure, rule, request, or, demand with which another must comply.

2. **Who** – the "who" to which the "what" is tasked or accountable is clearly understood and documented.

3. **When** – in respect to time lines, deadlines, due dates, etc.

4. **Where** – the environmental perimeters and geography within which an activity is addressed or completed.

5. **Why** – 'the' rules, regulations, and superior's directives.

6. **How** –in respect to the expected functionality of to do's.

*"Education is an admirable thing, but it is well to
remember from time to time that nothing that is worth
knowing can be taught."*
- Oscar Wilde

A leader moves beyond having mastered the multiple levels
of functionality of these letters, as they relate to one's
environment, and grasps the perspective of each letter that
truly aids in determining:

1. The growth necessary for individuals one leads, in
    order to build a high impact team and the level of
    comprehension of each letter by each employee.

2. Ownership of each letter must be conveyed and
    instilled within others for lasting results, so that the
    letters meaning becomes innate to everyone.

3. When to make allowances to any individual letter in
    attaining the ultimate goals and aims of the
    organization for sustained growth and profitability.

Leadership engagement from the five "W's" and one "H"
may serve as a successful benchmark for intervention,
whether constructive or critical in nature.

These six letters can serve as a template for facilitating
healthy dialogues, meetings, conferences, sales
presentations, training interventions, and social dialogue
with others in pursuit of keeping a strategic edge
(accelerate your leadership potential and that of your team,
visit www.KeepingTheEdge.com) among others in a
competitive business world today.

SECTION TEN:
Generational Connectedness

Chapter 33   Generational Connectedness: The Next Leadership Paradigm Shift to the Five Segmentations in Your Business

Chapter 34   Generational Connectedness: Unique Traits & Motivators of the Five Segmentations Within and Outside of Your Business

Chapter 35   Generational Connectedness: Future Challenges and Opportunities for Blending the Five Segmentations You Lead

Chapter THIRTY-THREE
Generational Connectedness:
The Next Leadership Paradigm Shift -
Moving Beyond Gender and Race to the
Next Managerial-Leadership Challenge
For Business and Organizational Success
and Working With the Five-Generational
Segmentations

"The problem with today's youth is that they lack direction,
commitment, and respect for their elders."
- Socrates

The evolution of managerial-leadership styles can be seen as a direct parallel to the evolution of both the business marketplace and culture in general. Decades of emphasis have heightened awareness of gender and race/ethnic sensitivities. Legally mandated actions deemed acceptable and unacceptable, regardless of the business practicality, have placed today's managers and leaders in a position of "standard operating policy" and behaviors.

While awareness and understanding of these protocols is not yet fully resolved (nor should there be less attention paid to these issues), the next real challenge and threat to organizational effectiveness is one that few realize. It will actually be more challenging than gender or race to overall leadership effectiveness: generational segmentation understanding.

Mandated rules of managerial-leadership sensitivity

*in the workplace, for sensitivity towards gender and
race/ethnicity, have been around for years, and
new to the paradigm is a larger basis for one's
actions in the workplace today -
generational segmentation!*

As an effective leader and member of an organization, moving past excuses, for one's station in life, is no secret to success. Now complicating these matters will be one's ability to recognize that we have, for the first time in recorded American workplace dynamics, very specific age groups.

There are five main "group-think" masses flowing throughout organizations. These age groups, in effect, make up five very different generational segmentations that directly influence how each operates, believes, and responds.

There is a direct and very defined connection between one's managerial-leadership style and one's age or generational segmentation. This is a greater obstacle to organizational effectiveness today than gender and race/ethnicity combined!

The five generational segmentations are:

1. **Centurions** – those making up the elder statesmen of the work force, ranging from 55 years of age and older. Census information suggests that there are some 55 million of these individuals in the workplace, with many comprising the most senior of leadership positions.

2. **Baby Boomers (and Eco Boomers)** – those making up the bulk of the middle ground, ranging from 38 to 55 years of age. Census information suggests that there are some 73 million of these individuals in the workplace, most with upwardly mobile career objectives.

3. **Generation X'ers** – those making up the more extreme and possession-oriented individuals of the work place. Ranging in age from late twenties to about 38 years, some 50 million individuals represent this demographic.

4. **Generation Y'ers** – those individuals that are post-college in age and entering the mainstream work force. Through about age 28, there are some 40 million occupants in this group.

5. **Generation MTV'ers (or Mosaic)** – those individuals just entering the work force as temporary, part-time workers, and interns. Typically about 16 to 21 years of age, this group comprises a staggering 55 million individuals or more.

To enhance your leadership ability and connectedness with others, approach each from the perspective of how that generational segmentation has been raised. To gain that perspective as a point-of-reference, simply consider what shared life experiences and opportunities have been afforded to that segmentation, based upon their generation.

As a leader, your ability to avoid rushing to the judgments of right-versus-wrong and good-versus-bad with individuals of differing generational segmentations will amplify your effectiveness. Merely engaging them from the operational generational segmentation style that is reflective of their age will distinguish you as a leader and not just another manager.

This truly becomes your means to generational connectedness: the next leadership paradigm shift.

Your ability to move beyond "gender and race" issues to the next managerial-leadership challenge for organizational success, working with the "five-generational segmentations," will add to your legendary leadership abilities!

Chapter THIRTY-FOUR
Generational Connectedness: Leading Different Generational Segmentations to Greatness Based Upon Their Unique Traits and Motivators

> *"The whole problem with the world is that fools and fanatics are always so certain of themselves, but wiser people so full of doubts."*
> *- Bertrand Russell*

The days of a wide-paintbrush-stroke approach to engaging individuals in an organization, as if they were crafted from the same mold, are gone.

The abilities to fluidly connect, understand, respect (not necessarily agree or disagree) ,and motivate the generational segmentations in a business organization will be the differentiators between greatness and significance. There is a direct and very defined connection between one's *personal* managerial-leadership style among others and one's age or generational segmentation.

This is also true for the methods by which managerial-leaders manage, lead, and engage others within business today. The "five generational segmentations" (*COACHING for IMPACT: The Art & Leadership Of Generational Coaching*, by Brown Books, ISBN# 0-9641240-3-3 /USA $29.95) can typically be identified as operating from these motivators:

1. **Centurions** – The 55 and older segmentation tends to be more structured, formal, regimented, reserved, focused, loyal, long-term oriented, purpose and value driven, organizationally committed ...

2. **Baby Boomers (and Eco Boomers)** – The 38 to 55 age segmentation tends to be less structured, more materialistic, change-resistant, more vocal and outgoing, commitment contingent, more loyal to an industry than a specific organization, title-driven, more formally educated ...

3. **Generation X'ers** – The 27 to 38 crowd tends to be more action-oriented, boundary-pushing, opportunity-driven, social/friend-oriented, change accepting, entitlement-driven, more instant-gratification-oriented ...

4. **Generation Y'ers** – The 21 to 28 segmentation has open minds but short attention spans, needs more diverse stimulation, is change-driven, technology savvy ...

5. **Generation MTV'ers (or Mosaic)** – The 16 to 21 segmentation is looking for purpose and valuable opportunity. Change is normal. They are relationship-driven, idealistic, technology-driven, highly socially conscious, short-term focused ...

To enhance one's leadership ability and connectedness with others, a leader should approach individuals from the perspective of how their generational segmentation likes to operate.

"We become who we have always been ...
Individuals typically operate outward
from our inward generational segmentation!"
- Jeffrey Magee

By fluidly engaging individuals, one-on-one or within a group, a leader can attain a higher level of individual performance and group effectiveness.

By continuously evaluating how individual segmentations operate, leaders can take the mystery and angst out of trying to determine how best to engage and motivate their team. They can reduce, if not eliminate, micro-management by merely delivering on the minimal needs of each segmentation and attaining maximum performance.

Chapter THIRTY-FIVE
Generational Connectedness: The Future Challenges and Opportunities For Blending the Five Segmentations You Lead For Effectiveness and Teaming

> *"I do not feel obliged to believe that the same God who has endowed us with sense, reason and intellect has intended us to forgo their use."*
> *- Galileo Galilei*

Managerial-leadership interventions, strategies, and tactics that served leaders well in the past will now prove counter-productive and, in some cases, even destructive with the diverse generational segmentations in today's business world.

The ability of leaders to find commonality among these five diverse generational segmentations and lead from that bound of connectedness will lead others to their potential greatness. The future challenges and opportunities for blending the five segmentations for effectiveness and teaming will become obvious the longer you keep yourself from blending individuals across generational segmentations as if they all operated similarly. Rather, the core mode of operation for each generational segmentation, is uniquely different today!

The "five generational segmentations" (*COACHING for IMPACT: The Art & Leadership Of Generational*

Coaching, by Brown Books, ISBN# 0-9641240-3-3 /USA $29.95) can become well-blended if each is respected for who they are, and if each is blended to compensate for one another's limitations and strengths for the sake of ultimate goal attainment. Each segmentation operates from the footprint left upon them as they have ascended through both their personal and professional lives. To create a cohesive team, consider drawing each in as follows:

1. **Centurions** – The 55 and older segmentation has a need to be appreciated and valued for their experienced perspective as the elder statesmen ...

2. **Baby Boomers (and Eco Boomers)** – The 38 to 55 segmentation has a need to be in charge and to be seen as the subject matter experts. They desire goal attainment ...

3. **Generation X'ers** – The 27 to 38 segmentation desires freedom, latitude to make independent decisions, control, maximum benefit, freedom to make choices en route to the goal ...

4. **Generation Y'ers** – The 21 to 27 segmentation prefers freedom to come and go as desired en route to goals, high participation in decision development strategies, opportunities to be creative and have fun in the execution stages of a decision ...

5. **Generation MTV'ers (or Mosaic)** – The 17 to 21 segmentation needs to feel the "why" to decisions and see that the immediate activities fit into the whole of where a business indicates that they are going. They need to feel appreciated and not taken for granted ...

As managerial-leaders in the business setting of today, pulling these seemingly different segmentations into one cohesive unit is critical to synergistic forward movement.

Cultivating a mindset that crosses all generational segmentations, encourages each to embrace learning from one another and encourages each to outwardly share among each other will ensure success today and survival tomorrow. Simultaneously, the elimination or conversion of any entity that hinders this is paramount to blending the generations and creating a spirit of teamwork.

Leaders and individuals that get this will get this. Those that continue to protect their domain at the expense of others will continue to face challenge, dysfunction, and turbulence!

"You craft your future based upon the present choices you make and execute!"
Jeffrey Magee

SECTION ELEVEN:
Controlled Risk-Taking

Chapter 36   Controlled Risk-Taking and Decision-Making: Facilitating the Decision Process Via the STOP Model©

Chapter 37   Controlled Risk-Taking and Decision-Making: Gaining Consensus and Buy-In Via the SMART Model©

Chapter 38   Controlled Risk-Taking and Decision-Making: Engaging the Four Core Stakeholders as Allies

Chapter 39   Controlled Risk-Taking and Decision-Making: Finding Optimal Quality and Determining When to Take Action

Chapter THIRTY-SIX
Controlled Risk-Taking and Decision-Making: Facilitating the Decision Process Via the STOP Model©

"Success is in the journey and not the destination. Managing risk and making sound decisions is in the steps of the journey ... "
- Jeffrey Magee

Separating the leaders from the followers is what many risk-laden decisions produce. Managing the levels of risk associated with known and unknown decisions in a business today can make the difference between a business expansion, market growth explosion, or an internal implosion.

Just as in producing the "thought leader" capacity within oneself and others, avoiding costly debates when risk is perceived may hamper effective decision-making activities necessary in risk scenarios.

A controlled decision-making matrix, used to ensure systematic forward decision facilitation in times of risk, is the "STOP Model©!"

Effective risk management decision-making comes partly out of an ability to facilitate the basic decision-making process. There are four basic steps to effective decision-making, which reduce and manage risk:

1. **(S) Stop and See** precisely what the challenge is, problem is, need is, subject matter for discussion is, the perceived risk factor to be addressed is. From this first step of addressing risk factor in the decision process, one's ability to singularly see the "what factor" will guide them to determine if the initially perceived risk element is worthy of continued engagement. Once that is determined, you can progress in the decision matrix, as there will no longer be a need to participate in step one activity.

2. **(T) Target and Think** precisely "why" that risk factor has been raised. Allow those engaged in the risk evaluation decision process to rationalize the "why factor" of the risk needing to be addressed now, later or never! It is in this vital step two that many times one becomes disproportionately sidetracked. Thus effective "thought processes" become derailed.

3. **(O) Organize Options** as to how best to proceed. This step directs you to invest the mental energies of you, and others around you, to explore and brainstorm viable solutions to the "risk item," which is being run through the four-step model. This step is critical for effective decision-making in the face of risk scenarios. It dictates that no action be initiated unless there are at least two viable options from which to select. This will ensure that a contingency plan, should the first application solution fail, has been considered and designed and is waiting to be deployed.

4. **(P) Pick and Proceed** with the option that is most viable. As a 'thought leader,' you will now be able to focus upon the decision process with the end always foremost in mind.

This model also affords managerial-leaders an objective instrument for cultivating involvement from a cross section of personalities, stake-holders, and subject matter experts in the pursuit of stimulating open and, when necessary, immediate decisions.

Facilitating the decision-making process with these four calculated steps aids in avoiding the dreaded pitfalls of one's inability to make a sound decision and take calculated risks. Common pitfalls:

1. Procrastination, out of which the 'Stop and See' step moves you.

2. Paralysis-of-Analysis, out of which the 'Target and Think' step moves you.

3. Fear, out of which the 'Organize Options' step moves you.

As a managerial-leader, this decision model allows for effective risk management facilitation by consciously addressing each step in the "**STOP Model©!**"

Chapter THIRTY-SEVEN
Controlled Risk-Taking and Decision-Making: Gaining Consensus and Buy-In Via the SMART Model©

"It can be very difficult to make significant changes,
especially when you have been in the habit of doing
things differently for decades, and especially when the
very success that brought you to the position you
now hold is rooted in doing some things, frankly,
the wrong way."
- W. Edwards Deming

Workers have learned four powerful excuses for minimal effort and maximum pay ... or put another way, people have learned to listen when being tasked for one of four openings that they can subsequently use to not participate.

Some individuals have been conditioned, raised, rewarded, and reared in environments that condoned, and even learned, how to get out of committing to work or participating mentally or physically with others. While done passively, their behavior is exceedingly aggressive.

Has another person ever given you reasons (really excuses) for not following through or completing an activity that was expected?

> 1. (Inhale of oxygen) Oh, I'm sorry, I did not realize that is "what" you wanted ....

2. (Inhale of oxygen) Oh, I'm sorry, I did not know (the "how" factors) I could use that, I can ….

3. (Inhale of oxygen) Oh, I'm sorry, I did not realize you needed it right now (the "when" factors), I can ….

4. (Exhale of oxygen) It wasn't realistic (the "why" factors); I had all of this other stuff to do ….

To non-combatively conversationally engage another person, in order to avoid confrontations at the back end of an engagement, for not completing that which was expected from them, consider the many applications of the **"Consensus Building Model"** called **"SMART©."**

And, with this conversational consensus-seeking model in your head, you can facilitate conversations, meetings, emails, and telephone conversations, using each letter as a checking system or list from which you can monitor whether or not feedback has been offered or whether a question is necessary to attain positive feedback.

The model directs managerial-leaders to seek consensus with others by communicating and seeking affirmative feedback to the:

1. *S - Specifics* of the subject matter, with respect to "what" one is discussing, needing, or expecting.

2. *M - Measurability* of "how" one is to proceed and/or what the expected and acceptable perimeters of the procedures are.

3. *A - Attaining Agreement* on each of the other four steps is the ultimate goal of the "SMART" model, and doing so conversationally is the primary objective.

4. *R – Realistic* perspective of whether the subject at hand is understood, believed, and valued, and whether the intended participant will be motivated to take action is the objective of this commitment step.

5. *T – Timeframe* of the intended subject matter needs to be nailed down as well. Any mini deadlines en route to the final completion should also be discussed and confirmed.

In facilitating any decision process, especially in risk-laden situations, use this model to hold yourself accountable to whether you're really committing to doing something or merely paying lip service to yourself. Failing to follow through on the action items you broadcast to your team sends a powerful message of mistrust.

Working with others, who constantly use excuses for nonperformance, can erode an otherwise healthy relationship or business. This model also serves as a powerful benchmark for whether an engagement with another person (child or adult, internal or external, customer, employee or boss …) is progressing toward success, productivity and, subsequently, profitability for the organization and its investors, or is merely another engagement en route to another dysfunctional encounter.

Gaining consensus and buy-in via the **"SMART Model©"** makes decision-making and risk-taking a controlled, manageable, SMART activity, and ensures increased net results every time.

Chapter THIRTY-EIGHT
Controlled Risk Taking and Decision Making:
Engaging the Four Core Stakeholders as Allies

"The task of the leader is to get his (her) people from where they are to where they have not been."
- Henry Kissinger

Managing the potential "veto" powers in the decision-making process is critical for sound decision-making and risk management control. Many times, it is the oversight of these four potential "Veto" stakeholders that causes increased risk in the decision-making process!

Whether you are engaged in critical self-thought or interacting with others, there are four sub-decisions to every overall decision. These four sub-decisions are especially noticeable when one makes decisions in environments or situations perceived to have an element of risk associated with them.

The four sub-decisions are critical stakeholders in the process and implementation of risk management decision-making protocols. Therefore, the *"Four Core Stakeholders"* of a decision, who need to be rallied and converted into advocates or allies, are:

1. ***Financial*** stakeholders scrutinize the decision from the perspective of what risks are associated with the decision financially.

2. ***Technical*** stakeholders scrutinize decisions from the perspective of what the decision delivers (or does not deliver), and what risks are associated.

3. ***User*** stakeholders are those individuals that will implement the decision and worry about how they will embrace, respond, or react to a decision, based upon their perceived level of risk associated with adhering to or avoiding the decision.

4. ***Coach/Advocate*** stakeholders are the people (or, at times, your internal voice) who, while they may not have a direct influence on a decision, can brief you on how to engage the other stakeholders to gain allies. This may be your internal voice that pushes you to buy something on impulse, causing you to later develop buyer's remorse when you reflect upon it from the vantage point of one of the other three stakeholders' perspectives.

Any non-addressed sub-decision can either derail implementation or be cause for a "veto" to be imposed upon a decision.

As an effective managerial-leader, don't get bogged down with whether there are four people, four teams, four committees, or multiple outside influencers involved in the decision process. Merely recognize, when making a decision, that there are varying levels of risk associated with every decision.

Engaging the four core stakeholders as allies simply involves the identification and engagement of each sub-decision: Financial; Technical; User; and Coach/Advocate.

Now you can control the level of risk by making sound thoughtful decisions that will increase your performance as a decision-maker and risk manager.

Chapter THIRTY-NINE
Controlled Risk-Taking and Decision-Making: Finding Optimal Quality and Determining When to Take Action

"Far better is it to dare mighty things, to win glorious triumphs, even though checkered by failure, than to take rank with those poor spirits who neither enjoy much nor suffer because they live in the gray twilight *that knows neither victory nor defeat."*
- *Theodore Roosevelt*

As a managerial-leader, controlling the levels of risk and determining the optimal quality to a decision is critical. It is especially critical today because leaders are faced with the balancing act of weighing long-term planning needs, while living in a short-term world.

One's ability to recognize at what point further analysis will bring about no greater resolution is paramount. Conversely, realizing that a decision made too hastily can bring about increased or new risks is also important.

Leaders excel, thrive, and live for identifying optimal quality decision-making opportunities. The following *"Risk Management Decision Model©"* will aid you in appropriately considering these variables. Consider these three measurement variables and for your environment:

1. Risk Levels
2. Complexity or Time Perimeters
3. Quality of Desired Decision

Visualize an L-grid (or draw one out as appropriate). In making a sound decision, measure two key variables on the L-grid. The vertical axis, from bottom/low to top/high, represents "RISK." The horizontal axis, from left/low to right/high, represents "COMPLEXITY/TIME."

Add an extra axis to this L-grid, starting from lower left corner, moving diagonally upward to the right hand corner. This axis will represent "QUALITY" of desired decision.

As you contemplate making any decision which carries a perceived "RISK" factor, realize that the highest level of "RISK" is typically associated with hastily made decisions. So, as one utilizes time as an ally or resource, the level of risk will decrease. Conversely, as more time is invested on decisions with complexity attached, the level of risk is expected to decrease and become more manageable.

To determine the "Optimal Quality" of a decision and at what point to initiate action, consider when these variables converge. Evaluate the axis lines to recognize:

1. When risk decreases as more time is invested in making a sound decision, there will come a point in which more time invested will actually begin to work against a good quality decision. This reverse bell curve implies that risk will once again increase.

2. Likewise, as more time is invested, the level of risk comes down and the quality increases. There too will become a point on the horizontal line where a bell curve develops and the quality will actually decrease if too much time is invested in the making and execution of a decision.

As a managerial-leader in your business today, the ability to make seamless and fluid decisions in the face of risk or not will distinguish you as a leader of stature. Arriving at "OPTIMAL QUALITY" in the face of "RISK" will ensure greater levels of efficiency, productivity and profitability and less turmoil with individuals.

Enhancing this net affect is the ability to transfer this skill and knowledge to each subsequent layer of "Thought Leaders" being cultivated within an organization or business. This then further propels success as a characteristic of an organization or business, through forward movement at every level and at every opportunity!

SECTION TWELVE:
Leadership Ethics

Chapter 40   Leadership Ethics: Seven Ethical Rules for Guiding Leadership Behavior

Chapter 41   Leadership Ethics: One's Character for Rent or Forecasted

Chapter 42   Leadership Ethics: Modeling it Daily

Chapter 43   Leadership Ethics: Legacy Factor

Chapter FOURTY
Leadership Ethics: Your Guidepost For Engagement

Seven Ethical Rules For Guiding Leadership Behavior Daily ...

"Your 'ethics' are those guideposts or rules which guide your actions, whether someone is watching you or not. Integrity is born out of these!"
- Dr. Jeffrey Magee,
Certified Management Consultant

The ethics of managerial-leadership greatness serve as a large umbrella under which one operates and serves others. Out from under this umbrella called "ethics" lie the traps and pitfalls of professional conduct today.

In the first years of this new century, the catastrophic crashes of significant businesses in America are directly rooted in the behaviors, actions, and mindsets of leaders who bastardized and sold their ethics in the final years of the last century.

To any learned observer, these managerial-leadership lapses are really no surprise. In fact, many of these tragedies in organizational leadership collapses, and even supposed business gurus, unmasked as charlatans, were already mentioned in several of my columns and writings – years before they actualized!

As detailed in the research of *COACHING for Impact: Leadership And The Art Of Generational Coaching* (ISBN # 0-9641240-3-3/US $29.95 Brown Book Publishers), it is reveled that sustained leadership effectiveness is demonstrated through very specific and consistent leadership behaviors. These behaviors are influenced or guided by very specific self-principles or rules. It is these shared rules that culminate in a *"Code of Ethics of Leaders!"*

Unwavering leaders do not allow their behaviors to be shaped by daily public opinion polls or what will necessarily gain the greatest immediate results at the expense of long-term needs. Non-Leaders realize that if they look "pretty," they can typically get away with these said actions. Leaders, however, are committed to attaining the highest standards of competence and performance from within themselves and from others.

In fact, a survey Gallup/UBS, reported in CFO magazine (August 2002 edition), indicates that among employees, "54 percent say they believe most corporate executives are honest and ethical; 59 percent say they aren't worth what they're paid," according to a poll by Gallup/UBS.

Consider these seven ethic guideposts as your *'Code Of Ethics of Leaders"* for determining your next course of mental and physical action:

1. **Competence** is being aggressively committed to the development of one's necessary skill set to compete competitively in the market place. Leaders recognize that their true differential in the marketplace is the human capital and their skill

assets. (*Training®* magazine, August 2002 edition, in a twenty-five year university study, reports that employees engaged in ongoing skill development trainings and opportunities earned, on average, 25 percent more than their colleagues.)

2. **Accountability** for cultivating strong networks within their organization and business for greater community.

3. **Integrity** driven by constant vision, goals, and objectives, consistent with the overall Code of Ethics that others know that your actions will be consistent, whether one's Grandmother was in the room or not!

4. **Professional Responsibility and Duty** to the dictated organization or business expectations.

5. **Respect for Rights and Personal Dignity** of others. Gage actions against this point to ensure that individuals are not expected to violate this at their personal gain.

6. **Commitment to The Other Person** as a beacon for other person vested.

7. **Social Responsibility** via a sense of commitment to the community in which one works and lives.

These seven ethical standards serve as benchmark behaviors of managerial-leadership greatness. One's leadership ethics and the foundation essence of leadership integrity, which guide engagement actions with colleagues and customers and serve as models for what is expected from future leaders, resonate outward from these seven *"Code of Ethics of Leaders"* today.

Chapter FOURTY-ONE
Leadership Ethics: Is Your Character for Sale or is it Reliable?

"Always do what is right: this will gratify some of the people and astonish the rest."
- Mark Twain

If you have it and others know it, then it can be relied on. If not, then yours is probably for sale to the highest buyer.

The "it" is your ethics, derived from the Greek word 'ethos,' which means character.

From the beginning of time, ethics have been equated with character, and character is a key measurement of leadership. Ethics, whether personal or organizational, are inextricably linked to one's character.

Hence, one's ethics drive one's character, and that is best demonstrated by how one defines who they are and what they are all about in life.

In evaluating some of the replicable influencers that have crafted your professional operating ethics as a leader, create a business inventory of sequential contact centers-of-influence that may serve as a model in the development of your present and future leaders.

Some of those influencers may have been and can subsequently be:

1. Cross-cultural business experiences.

2. Participation among different departments and committees served on.

3. Stakeholders engaged and learned from.

4. Organizational mentors cultivated.

5. Accountability levels attained.

6. Commitment levels demonstrated.

7. Conflicts successfully navigated professionally.

8. Experiencing taking stands against popular opinions that ended in positive resolution.

9. Knowing and doing what is right when no one is present to observe you.

As a leader, well-defined ethics from which one can find solace and operational behaviors are a defining difference between getting by and thriving. In the past decade, one has to go back nearly the entire decade for a standout example of leadership ethics at work, with people watching or not.

The night air was cold, the sky bright and the business was New England's Malden Mills. CEO Aaron Fuerenstein had seen his family's "Polartec" fleece from its textile mill completely burn to the ground. Taking his $300 million dollars in insurance, he paid all of his employees their entire salaries while the plant was rebuilt. He could have taken his money and run. His comments in 2002 looking backward: "The God of money has taken over to an extreme our business leaders' decisions ... I paid the salaries because it was the right thing to do!"

This is not the only reference point of the past decade, but it does powerfully reflect that, as a leader, your every action rises to the level ethically powerful. What appears to be epidemic across many businesses today is the level of arrogance, which is only surpassed by the level of functional illiteracy, of many individuals vested with leadership positions.

A leader knows the depth of intellectual, emotional, and ethical wealth within him or herself, and they only draw upon that which they know they posses.

So what maps guide your actions when no one is present to see you?

Chapter FOURTY-TWO
Leadership Ethics: Modeling It Daily! The Bottom Line is a Matter of Choice.

"I have learned that when I make an immediate [choice], I am correct 60 percent of the time. And when I deliberate significantly, I am correct 70 percent of the time. I have learned that it is not worth the additional 10 percent, and people know then what to expect from me."
- Merrill Lynch

Greatness in executive leadership is measured by the quality of a leader's decisions and his or her commitment to such choices. From among the masses, leaders emerge according to their choices made and executed within a business.

Every choice a person makes has internal and external consequences. Internal consequences are related to a leader's ethics. An ethical decision strengthens a leader's moral resolve and influences subsequent decisions. These choices then broadcast to one's team a standard of decision-making—what is expected of them, what is unacceptable and what will be rewarded.

Choices reveal (whether consciously or unconsciously) a leader's bottom line, his or her underlying system of values that determines the following:

1. The level of self-responsibility for which one is willing to be held accountable.

2.   The eagerness to strive toward meaningful goals.

3.   The willingness to be held accountable to such goals.

4.   The desire to be intentionally aware of one's location and direction in relation to future goals.

5.   The drive to make decisions in an ethical and reliability manner.

6.   Recognition of the importance of common sense in decision-making.

As a leader, you should assess your proficiency and integrity at decision-making. One way to do this is to evaluate those on your team and their skill at decision-making. People tend to emulate their leaders.

There is a critical ethical dilemma in business today, caused by the rise of individuals with a minimal-effort-for-maximum-pay mentality. This toxic attitude may be the greatest potential setback to growth, community and prosperity for the coming business cycle because as it permeates every functional level of an organization, such behavior perpetuates an erosion of leadership ethics.

A leader's choices should focus on long-term consequences. The realization that the immediate outcome of a decision matters very little in comparison with the long-term consequences should inspire responsible decision-making on the part of a leader and respect and emulation on the part of a team.

As a leader, your ability to demonstrate "choice-fullness" in your actions will tacitly communicate your ethics as an individual and business leader, compelling others to greatness!

The benchmark of morality and ethical actions has been abdicated, abolished, and excused. What is your bottom line? Do your long-term, ethical decisions inspire others to strive for greatness?

Chapter FOURTY-THREE
Leadership Ethics: Legacy Factor!
Three Core Elements of Greatness

"A leader should be able to provide to others:
Hope, Vision, and Forward Movement!"
- John Shiroma, Executive Vice President,
The United States Junior Chamber Of Commerce

Excellent leaders within businesses, associations, and volunteer organizations leave lasting legacies, not only because of what they do while they are present, but because of what continues to happen after they have departed!

The belief systems and core principles resonating within an individual and guiding their actions when no one is present can be called one's Operating Leadership Ethics. Many leaders' rock solid ethics are the cause of their lasting legacies.

If you were to search the annals of history for those individuals that have been deemed true leaders, you would typically find people who were possibly controversial in their generation, but were unshakeable in their moral outlook. These individuals did not allow themselves to be influenced by the popular opinion poll of the day in order to satisfy their need for approval; they refused the temptation of reckless disregard for the future, which so often, unfortunately, accompanies those in power.

In far too many businesses and organizations today, the prevalence of infighting, self-serving strategies, and opportunistic tactics among leaders is shocking.   One reason for this is the widespread lack of fundamental leadership ethics; a result is the loss of countless long-term business opportunities.

To leave a lasting leadership legacy one should consider how to foster, incorporate, and exemplify the following three Core Factors:

1. **The Hope Factor** – How does a leader's every comment, action, choice, engagement of others, and environmental support action stimulate a sense of hope within others to reach toward greatness today and tomorrow?

2. **Vision Factor** – Do the leader and his or her leadership team have the ability to craft, articulate, and support a focus, view, or vision of where the team has the ability to grow?

3. **Forward Movement Factor** – Net results are brutal, unambiguous measurements of where one is and where one is going. As a leader, your every decision and action has net results: each one stifles your team, maintains it, or helps it to grow!

The greatest impediment to future leadership legacies is the posturing, politicking, and rivalry that occur when a group of potential high-impact leaders lose focus of their real purpose as leaders!

When a person gambles away their leadership ethics,
the legacy is never flattering!

This can be seen across the nation every day in the leadership gatherings designed to lay out the future growth of an organiza tion. Typically, "future growth" is a misnomer, and the true legacy of the company is one of squandered opportunities, squelched ideas, lost hope, and absent vision. Why? The leaders aren't being leaders.

A person's self-ethics evolve into one's leadership ethics, which guide every choice and action made for the sake of a company. Are you developing your talent bench of prospects to assume tomorrow's leadership needs? Are you making ethical decisions and imparting the importance of ethics to your team? This is the true legacy of leadership and a reflection of one's greatness. (If you would like to learn more about the leadership ethics models of today's high performance leaders, make sure to check out *COACHING for Impact: Leadership And The Art Of Generational Coaching*, page 87, ISBN # 0-9641240-3-3/US $29.95, Brown Book Publishers.)

A leader with committed ethics is dedicated to the development of his or her own inner strength as a servant of their team. Here are five fast-track methods that feed a legendary leader's legacy of Vision, Hope, and Momentum:

1. A leader reads both fiction and non-fiction works on a regular basis to glean upcoming trends, new ideas, and long-term insight. (The Book-of-the-Month Club reports the average adult does not read even one non-fiction book from cover-to-cover each year.)

2. A leader subscribes to content-rich monthly periodicals.

3. A leader regularly engages in educational and skill development workshops, retreats, symposiums, and classes.

4. A leader freely shares action-oriented, visionary ideas with others.

5. A leader mentors many high-capacity performers and invests liberally into them.

With this continual emersion into growth-oriented knowledge, information, and experience, a leader creates an environment conducive to the development of others and contributes to a flourishing organization. (Explore www.KeepingTheEdge.com as a continuum of leadership self-development.)

With continual refinement of your intellectual leadership net worth, you can ensure that everyone within your sphere of influence is energized and working in the same direction. You must ensure that everyone is working from the same **MAP©** (Mental Action Plan©), which in the business world, is referred to as a Value or Mission Statement.

Here is a fast and efficient six-step template to use in crafting the MAP© for your team. With your stakeholders on board, take a piece of paper and answer each prompt:

1. Who?
2. What?
3. When?
4. Where?
5. Why?
6. How?

Once you and your team have developed a clear, cogent response to each of these prompts, everyone will know the goals to which they are striving. They can now independently gauge all actions, reactions, and decisions against a common template and work toward a common goal.

For a true leader, today does not matter as much as tomorrow. Too often the urgent supersedes the truly important, but a great leader avoids this pitfall by planning for and investing in the future.

Having a foundation of operating ethics, ensuring that the legacy you have planted and nurtured will be harvested by others!

SECTION THIRTEEN:
Loyalty Advantage

Chapter 44   Loyalty Advantage: Becoming Other Person Centered

Chapter 45   Loyalty Advantage: Increasing Loyalty With Others

Chapter 46   Loyalty Advantage: Moving Beyond Blame

Chapter FOURTY-FOUR
Loyalty Advantage:
Becoming Centered on Other People
to Foster Loyalty as a
Successful Leader

"Thinking is hard work. That is why so few people
engage in it – practice it!"
- Henry Ford

Leaders have long since been confronted with the question of how best to build and maintain the loyalty of the individuals for whom they are accountable and responsible. Many times this question is a source of much debate.

In today's competitive business world, the key to finding that unique and individual variable within each member in an organization—the variable that serves as a catalyst for loyalty toward the leadership—is all about the leader becoming centered upon the other person.

Most organizations today have invested significant time, energy and financial resources into building what they believe and expect will incur loyalty. If the members of such organizations don't respond in kind with the expected level of loyalty and commitment, the organizational leaders become indignant.

Traditional "groupthink" attempts to create loyalty among employees typically include any of the following:

1. Enhanced compensation benefits packages.

2. Empowering work environments.

3. Ergonomic workspaces.

4. Union-friendly facilities.

5. Above average salary or wages.

6. Engaging social activities, events, functions, etc.

7. Fast-tracked and compounded vacation time.

8. Consistent on-the-job performance bonuses, perks, awards, rewards, etc.

9. Ongoing educational, and skill-development opportunities.

To truly address this issue, you must step outside the "groupthink" approach and become centered on your team members, one person at a time. You may find that what determines an individual's Loyalty Advantage may be far less than you would expect.

To determine how best to address an individual's loyalty, consider the following formula:

Loyalty= **Needs** met according to an individual's
Expectations

The number of instances where organizations implode or experience dysfunction due to loyalty issues is significant. Even situations in which leaders have painstakingly designed exhaustive programs in order to build, grow, and drive loyalty of employees, they have failed to develop the allegiance of their team members!

To become more focused on those in your company (and in the process, earn their trust), try this leadership drill. Write the name of each of your direct reports and do the following:

1. List what you believe to be their top five expectations of you and the organization.

2. List your perceptions of their top five professional and personal needs, which drive them to be on your team and at your location daily.

3. Flip over this sheet of paper, sit down with each individual, and have him or her give responses to the same two questions.

4. Now compare your answers.

Building the Loyalty Advantage starts with understanding the needs and expectations of each individual, and then determining whether you can address and fulfill those needs. And with today's workplace being increasingly diverse in culture, ethnic origin, and generational segmentation, leaders will also find that there may be very few actions that work among all groups to build loyalties!

In many instances, business leaders may realize that what it takes to build loyalty with individuals is far less than what is traditionally offered, and is more cost effective to the organization.

Chapter FOURTY-FIVE
Loyalty Advantage:
Increasing Loyalty from Others
as a Leader

"Which came first, the chicken or the egg?"
- Unknown

Business leaders, employees, and labor unions have long since struggled with one question: Should the loyalty of employees merit acts of reinforcement and repayment on the part of the leadership, or should leaders provide benefits and bonuses in order to build loyalty?

The struggle centers on whether loyalty should be expected in a business setting or whether it is to be earned by the leadership. If it is to be earned, how does one earn it—or lose it?

A recent *JMI Loyalty Survey©,* of more than 1,000 professionals in Fortune 100 firms, the United States Military and several major associations, found that the elements necessary to building a Loyalty Advantage among team members were usually basic workplace requirements.

What do people seek from their leaders in order to earn their loyalty? Consider the top responses to this question:

1. Knowing that they are **appreciated** through regular feedback from both their immediate manager-leader and their organization.

2. Tangible evidence of **their ideas being sought after**, considered, and occasionally acted upon.

3. Management **maintaining the confidences shared with them** by members of that organization and not spreading gossip.

4. Consistent and **fair treatment** of all players on a team.

5. Knowing that **management (leaders) will defend them** in a crunch, if a situation is not a violation of ethics, procedure, or law, should the organization take odds with one of their acts.

6. Knowing that their manager-leader has an **unwavering foundation of honesty**.

7. Trusting in them to do their assigned work and **avoid micro-management** interventions.

8. Feeling that they are being **compensated fairly** (not necessarily above market) for what they do in comparison to others in their marketplace.

9. Knowing that the **organization keeps them informed** on growth trends and business issues critical to their life and position, and does not generate a sense that they are being purposefully kept in the unknown.

10. That they can trust their leaders and that the **leaders don't lie, mislead,** or act in self- serving manners.

11. That organizations **continually offer skill-development** opportunities to make individuals valuable players to the team.

As a business leader, building a Loyalty Advantage will be invaluable in building a cohesive team and curbing turnover, attrition, and dissention among members. This will also aid in generating a sense of security among members, and this unity allows all involved to evolve to a greater level of awareness and efficiency. Now the leader moves to a position of organizational facilitator of needs, rather than a manager or leader of the elements that feed these needs.

Here's a reality check: to determine if your actions as a leader work to increase loyalty among your team or, in fact, destroy it, do the following:

1. Write down the names of all of your direct reports.

2. Now benchmark each of the above 10 questions and note how they relate both individually to each name and overall for all names.

Evidence reveals that when an individual's real needs and real expectations are met, their loyalty increases exponentially. As a leader, you need to examine your daily actions with individuals and groups against the above list. In doing so, you will be able to determine if your daily behaviors earn the loyalty of your colleagues or not.

Chapter FOURTY-SIX
Loyalty Advantage:
Moving Beyond Blame Toward Togetherness

"The excuse factory runneth over..."
- Stanley Squirm
(Fictional character from SQUIRM to LEARN)

There is no loss for excuses when it comes to the question of why people cannot coexist, partner, and stay professional in the business place.

You may have heard some of the following excuses before:

1. That won't work.

2. Why can't we do it the way we always have?

3. We have a special situation here, and you don't understand.

4. We tried that once before.

5. You can't do that here.

6. That is not my job description.

7. I was not hired to do that/this ....

8. I am the only one here that ever ...

9. We should not do anything until …

10. I don't have to!

11. I should have been promoted, not that …

With every excuse that is not constructively addressed, you can see and feel the loyalty level decline within an organization. To compound this, the more this incident occurs unchallenged by management-leadership, the more loyalty, which may have been present, toward the leader begins to plummet!

As reported in *CEO PERSPECTIVES®*, a supplement to *CHIEF EXECUTIVE OFFICER magazine 2002*, "Among the host of challenges chief executives face at the start of the 21st century, none rank higher than issues relating to the workplace of the future." The survey article also references that leading the concerns of chief executives will be finding, training and keeping qualified workers. The actual workforce is decreasing, becoming more ethnically diverse and less male-dominated; it will be greatly compounded by a significant skill gap among all of the workers.

Additional research actually reveals that at the root of many imploding situations and breakdowns in loyalty is the pattern that most companies are matching up their lowest-paid resources (with the least skill-development base) with their most valuable assets: customers. It's an obvious fact, but no one seems to acknowledge it.

Recognizing that there are myriad reasons for individuals to feel compelled to blame others for business problems their station in life, the leader must have the mettle to move beyond the blame-game, animosity, and negativity, and move others toward resolution, solution and accomplishment. If not, blame can become institutionalized and cancerous to a business, new colleagues, and thriving business success.

To do this, an effective leader may consider the following:

1. How quickly to transition interactions from focusing on loyalty-busting issues, such as right-versus-wrong and good-versus-bad, to more fruitful lines of thought.

2. How to focus energies on moving individuals toward collaborative healthy questions, engaging and non-threatening dialogue and multiple viable alternatives.

By being consistent and persistent, a leader can create an atmosphere where blame isn't used as a motivator. Once this new climate is attained, leaders will find that people tend to come together instead of grow apart!

SECTION FOURTEEN:
Entitlement Mentality

Chapter 47	Entitlement Mentality: The Creation of One's Own Problem Child
Chapter 48	Entitlement Mentality: Eroding a Team, One Me'ism at a Time
Chapter 49	Entitlement Mentality: Working for FAIR, not EQUAL, Playing Status

Chapter FOURTY-SEVEN
Entitlement Mentality:
The Creation of One's Problem Child,
Growing the Entitlement Mentality
From Birth to Retirement

"Entitlement in the work place is a collision of two
peoples...perspective of how the 'old times' versus the
'young group' see things and expectation levels are set."
- Roger Herman
Fellow, The Institute of Management Consultants

We are living in a business world that we have all actively created. From management and labor unions to employees and parents, the challenge to remain relevant in the business world today requires a radical shift from what was (and that was OK) to what must be. We have now discovered that the business model in which many workers grew up in the 1980s and 1990s was grossly misleading. This phantom reality lead to many people having expectations of the work place that simply cannot be sustained in today's reality.

The test of true leadership from the management and labor side of a business will be seen in today's business reality. The survivability of a business can be equated to the blood flow of a human being. All business is, at its most elementary level, dependent upon the flow of revenues. The flow of revenue to a business is like the flow of blood to a person; them healthier the blood, the greater survivability that entity has. The more that entity hemorrhages blood or has limited blood flow, the weaker that entity becomes. Today, business revenues are being placed into jeopardy and becoming greatly hindered by the continuation of people focusing on entitlements, rather than the question of how we get our businesses back to a sustainable, healthy level.

In the 1990s, it appeared as if everything was plentiful, anything could be attained, no one was held accountable for his or her actions and individuals saw themselves as a personnel asset to be sold to the highest bidder. This was further compounded by actions that jobs would be protected by big brother – otherwise known as labor unions and government – even when the position no longer served as a viable part of a healthy business.

An online survey of the top 300 Certified Speaking Professionals and leading business leadership consultants, leading Keynotes and Training interventions across America today, revealed insight as to this issue of leadership challenge today, in respect to entitlement issues – over the following four chapters, those findings will be detailed.

In order for business leaders to begin to effectively and non-combatively address the entitlement mindset that's eroding businesses today, one must realize the varied reasons why we have arrived where we are today, and how the differing generational segmentations view this concept?

"When jobs are plentiful, employees use entitlement to get and keep what they want. In other words, a power tool in a market where employees had the upper hand ... and this manifested itself with large companies. Now, attitudes must change, and a realistic view of the business marketplace must prevail as people realign to remain in business. Training employees to treat a company as their own will be key," said Kristine Sexter, former vice president of Robert Half & Associates (employee recruiters) and today an executive leadership trainer with WorkWise.

Contributing to this entitlement challenge today is a decade of over compensation of workers in order to attract and keep quality employees. In the last years of the 1990s, signs within both the economy and business infrastructure began to unravel.

Labor Department announcements in *TIME®* indicate that for the Fourth Quarter 2002, professionals, managers, and technical and administrative workers now make up 43 percent of the unemployed. When employees are reluctant to reconfigure their compensation packages to bring them into alignment with business realities today, they ultimately displace themselves.

In the fall 2001, the employees of Southwest Airlines initiated an across-the-board pay cut to ensure all their colleagues maintain employment in the face of adverse market trends in the post 9-11 airline industry. Southwest is the only airline in the post 9-11 economy to post consecutive profits for the following twelve months!

Another factor in entitlement challenges for leaders is from the mix of how generational segmentations' perspectives in the work place are shaped.

Tulsa-based psychologist, Dr. Jay Kent-Ferraro, Co-Author of *COACHING For IMPACT: The Art Of Generational Leadership,* takes a much more critical look at what faces business leaders and workers. The past two decades have delivered a workplace where people have become comfortable – we live in the most under-sacrificed and overindulged culture that has ever walked the earth. Unawareness of any substantive sacrifices has resulted in a character flaw within the modern psyche, namely, "I am, therefore I deserve." This has birthed a crisis of meaning with no purpose or reason. In the absence, many people fill this void with greed and satiation of material consumption and relational excesses (e.g. Enron, Tyco), to name a few. Thus the "I am, therefore I deserve" ethos has culminated in a sense of deserving for a job attempted, done or done well.

Compounding this even further is labor unions stirring the emotions of entitlements, without reflection on the short and long-term ramifications to its initiatives. Witness an October 2002 *USA TODAY*® newspaper reporting the International Union of Electronic Workers-Communication Workers of America pushing for GE employees to go on strike, should GE go forward with an increase in employee co-payment participation for its company-provided health benefits, from 10 percent to 15 percent. Without regard to the significant increase in health increase premium payments, businesses are expected to pay to provide employees this premium service!

To counter this momentum and stay healthy and market-relevant, business leaders should:

1. Revaluate all expenditures, investments, activities, benefits, sponsorships and endeavors, and re-cost justify them using today's standards, not those of yesterday. Fixed dollars, associated with what a business is supposed to be about (product or service

sector production/offerings), must be evaluated first.

2. Then, detail the quality of live and employee entitlements. From this massive list and the associated costs, a report should be internally publicized for all to take ownership. In times of crises and radically changed scales-of-economy, information, and open dialogue are critical to survival and prosperity.

Many times a leader can gain buy-in and heightened levels of commitment from everyone in the business by sharing the reality of the financial picture. Increased innovation and reinvention of appropriate opportunities can come out of this entitlement mindset, created from yesterday, by designing open and active creative design teams today.

Many times, people do not really understand how much entitlements add up. When confronted with maintaining all of the entitlements, with the reality of someone loosing their job, or negotiating away some to maintain the health of the business and increased opportunities for all to maintain their employment, people may impress you.

Physical evidence of entitlement is indisputable.
It doesn't have an agenda for business growth,
an attitude for organizational behavior success,
nor an opinion of togetherness.
It is precisely that – fact!

Chapter FOURTY-EIGHT
Entitlement Mentality:
Eroding a Team, One Me'ism at a Time

"Companies have caused people to focus more on what the company is or is not doing for the employee than what the employee should be doing for the company."
- David Cobb,
Former Executive WorldCom/MCI

The "Company Town" syndrome of the past century has given way to the "Me Town" of this new century!

Entitlement raises its head in many forms in the workplace today. With the collision of differing generational segmentations' operating beliefs and ethics, culture conditioning, EEOC regulations, never-ending government policies regarding what an employer can and cannot do and what must be financially incurred and offered, it does not take long before a systemic "entitlement mentality" is created – and continually reinforced in the work place.

Today, younger workers arrive on the job with unbridled enthusiasm and a desire to attain greatness immediately. They learn by reading, and not necessarily having done it; they become restless quickly. More seasoned workers have been raised with a mindset that one must put in his or her time to ascend, and on-the-job experience is essential for success.

Further complicating organizational greatness and a sense of teaming or collective togetherness has become a prevailing worker mentality of accepting a functional position within an organization in this free-market economy (of which far too many don't comprehend), and then expecting that workplace environment to begin making allowances to accommodate them. And when this is not met, instead of leaving with their free will, and taking their talent assets to another employer or, better yet, starting their own business, passive-aggressive performance behavior appears, litigation commences, or even worse outcomes take place.

The **"Me'ism Entitlement Mindset"** appears in a number of ways:

1. I am here; therefore, you should pay for my continued education, without my commitment to remain with you.

2. I should receive some sort of bonus or perk upon successful completion of any advanced degrees and/or certifications.

3. I should be paid a premium for my labor, and I am entitled to regular pay increases forever, regardless of performance or health of the organization.

4. I should be provided with what have become standard benefits, like health insurance (medical, eye, dental, and drug prescription), and at minimal or no participating financial participation. Also, this should be further extended to my family and spouse or significant other.

5. I should be provided paid time off within my first year of employment, regardless of contribution and performance to my employer.

6. I should be given paid time off for days when I am sick. Also, I can use it honestly or misleadingly – tough stuff for my colleagues and employers. ??

7. I should also be able to accept others' accrued time if I run out of mine.

8. I should be offered a retirement vehicle, which my employer puts in money if I do.

9. I should have input on what the workplace environment looks like and what ergonomically correct furnishing are made available for me to access and perform my job.

10. I should be able to decide my work assignments and set my own work hours; hours that accommodate my lifestyle, regardless of the customer's lifestyle or needs.

11. If I decide to stop working for an employer, I can just not show up; no need for a two-week notice.

12. My opinion should be sought on decisions, even if I have no vested interest or financial ownership.

13. If I don't like something, I can just walk away; someone else will take care of it.

14. That which is not my direct responsibility, I can abdicate away and not be expected to aid others in need.

15. I should be able to mix my personal life and life choices with my workplace environment, and no one should be able to comment on that.

As a leader, these expectations today cause substantial internal conflicts.

It is one's spirit of leadership effectiveness or ineffectiveness that will enable one to realign the people forces to recognize, in the new economy, which offerings can be supported, which offerings should be linked to true performance attainments, which offerings are "entitled" and which ones are true gifts to be appreciated, and when not appreciated, should be reduced, altered or eliminated.

Some of the engagement dialogues a leader must be prepared for, and which a leader must facilitate with all organizational members:

1. It is not to suggest that any one of these **"Me'ism Entitlement Mindset"** examples is fair or unfair, right or wrong, good or bad. It does raise the dialogue, with all of these entitlement expectations, how a leader should address each constructively when raised by employees.

2. Also, how they are addressed when one employee raises a new expectation and ties it to others already being offered.

3. When an employee raises new entitlements, being offered to new arrivals in a work place that the veterans feel they had to work years to attain.

4. To remain relevant employees, labor unions and leaders will have to come together and examine whether these entitlements can be further supported, increased or reduced.

An effective leader can get to the heart of how to engage and motivate members of their team. They can gradually work to remove the **"Me'ism Entitlement Mindset"** and determine a working list of what may be short term and long-term motivators and incentives from each subset of employees and generational segmentation of employees by having each individual employee:

1. On a piece of paper, write your name and the decade generation (i.e., I am in my 20s, 30s, 40, 50s, etc.) you represent. Under that heading, list all of the specific things that they would perceive as incentives that would cost no actual hard dollars.

2. On the reverse of that sheet of paper, list perceived incentives that may have a fixed dollar amount.

Form this list, then scrutinize for commonality among all workers. Realize that what employees today may recognize as entitlements or incentives for increased work ethic and commitment may be substantially different than what management has come to expect based upon yesterday.

The effective leader, who leaves a lasting legacy of greatness, will be able to move these forces to synergistically come together.

Chapter FOURTY-NINE
Entitlement Mentality:
Working For FAIR, Not EQUAL
Playing Status

"Far too many people are legends within their own mind!"
- Unknown

A mind shift must be addressed as to what is "fair" and how to establish a working understanding that all people are "not created equally" when it comes to the business marketplace.

This premise is sure to get people excited. As a leader, it is paramount to the survival of an organization and the development of all players that individuals recognize that being treated fairly is not same as being treated equally.

To make this critical business adjustment for the actual survival and growth of a business of tomorrow, two radical adjustments must be made today:

1. A determination of the true net value of an organization must be affixed to each player. This will be a very unpopular move; for managers this will cause debate, and for true leaders, this will be comprehended.

2. A cultural and generational paradigm shift will have to be undertaken, whereby a person no longer receives entitlements for hanging on for years or living the longest

within an organization. Nor can entitlements be handed out based solely and independently upon an individuals gender, race, educational credentials, ability to impact bottom line, who one knows, or merely being fortunate enough to be born into a family lineage of previously accomplished individuals. Instead, "all" of the variables must be balanced and blended into one final determination!

A true leader knows the power of humility and the necessity of treating all people with dignity and respect - FAIR. This is devoid of necessitating treatment of all individuals within an organization, whereby all players must be treated EQUALLY.

From a business mindset, individuals are not equal, as employees deliver differing levels of profitability to an organization.

To attain a FAIR relationship with others, "Scales-of-Economy" must be established among all members of an organization. Lessons learned from the embattled airline industry after 2000 can assist in understanding this variable clearer. Let's say the CEO earns hundreds-of-thousands of dollars, and, with bonuses, can top a million dollars in annual compensation. Down the line, a flight attendant is paid $50,000.00 or more for working half months each month. Consider what a pilot must earn, and do the same for all employees system-wide. The answer to the misguided state of reality is "entitlement," as each person actually believes they are worth that financial variable to their respective organization!

Once an employee is over compensated, it is very difficult to get them to understand the reality of where their salary should have been all along, based upon these "Scales-of-Economy".

Leaders must open lines of communication with stakeholders in an organization and encourage open dialogue among all leaders down line from them with their respective teams. This line of communication must allow for two-way dialogue and must share with employees the reality of the budgets and profitability benchmarks, as well as how an organization works.

As a leader, it will be challenging to accomplish this mindset shift today, given the range of conditioning with which people today arrive:

1. My parents always rescued me from authority figures (teachers, school administrators, neighbors, other parents, government officials, etc.) and, thus, excused my behavior and rewarded me daily for merely waking up.

2. I was paid beyond minimum wage at an earliest of age in the work place, so above-scale compensation is a norm.

3. Society at its highest level does not hold individuals accountable for actions. It provides daily examples through the media of behaviors being excused and presented as all people are "created equal," which must mean we are all entitled to the same rewards and awards, regardless of effort, participation and accomplishment.

4. You see this abdication of self-responsibility across all ages within society today, and this permeates into business structures as well. Consider the elder that fakes being handicapped to gain pre-access to businesses, airline flights and parking, yet is exceedingly capable when the reason for misrepresentation subsides. It is a belief system of "I am better than everyone else and, thus, entitled."

5. An adversarial relationship between labor unions and management over the decades (and in many cases justly warranted) has produced a systemic belief that labor is "entitled" to more and more,

From a leadership perspective, people are not equal. People do not bring parity to business in terms of their abilities, talents and dedication. Entitlement must be replaced with objective quantifiable performance accomplishment rewards, compensation, and lifestyle awards.

Consider the environment and culture that a leader creates as that organization's DNA. This DNA will dictate how these forces either come together and work for a healthy structure within an organization or how these forces will implode and lead toward greater organizational dysfunction. Change the DNA, and "entitlement" mentality can subside; otherwise, "entitlement" will most surely be the cancer that kills off organizational effectiveness!

SECTION FIFTEEN:
Assessment Instruments

Chapter 50	Assessment to Success: Interviewing for Impact and Building Winning Teams
Chapter 51	Assessment To Success: What Gets Measured, Gets Measured

Chapter FIFTY
Assessment to Success:
Interviewing For Winning Teams

"It starts with recruiting selection and orientation.
It is easier to train an eagle then to teach a pig to fly!"
Mel Kleiman
(mkleiman@humetrics-inc.com)

As a legendary leader, building a winning team from the beginning can make leading a winning team much easier.

In most business realities today, managerial-leaders assume their positions and, thus, their teams. When an opportunity presents itself to add a complimenting player to a team, management most often fumbles this opportunity.

Many times, the newly acquired player is not objectively acquired as a "personnel asset" that truly compliments and adds to the pre-existing team's strengths by filling an existing team's weaknesses. The new player is often a shade of what already exists.

Further complimenting this endeavor is management's frequent hurried approach to fill a vacancy. This lack of thorough objective analysis complicates the process of advertising, interviewing, and adding a new player to a team.

Consider the use of the following template for your determination of what your next "personnel asset" must have, and would be nice if they had as they arrive to your team.

Your **"Personal Performance Interview Assessment Instrument"** should have three basic sections:

1. First, start with a mindset that, for every functional position you seek, you must craft a new assessment instrument for that position. Some qualifiers may blend over from one position to another, but each position has unique functions, and those should be detailed and measured.

    So, with this understanding for every position, list that specific position on the top of a page. Adjacent to that "Position Statement," note the basic expected functions and tasks that a candidate will be expected to execute. Down the CENTER of the page, list each necessary **"Trait Competency/Behavior/ Skill"** a person must possess in order to be capable to execute that function or task.

2. Second, on the LEFT side of the page, adjacent to each entry, place a measurement scale of numbers, one through five. This scale is for **"Importance of Skill Level Sought"** for that position (1=Not Required; 2=Nice To Have; 3=Basic Requirement Needed; 4=Important; 5=Key).

3. On the RIGHT side of the page, adjacent to each entry, place a measurement scale of numbers, one through five. This scale is for **"Candidate's Skill Level Possession"** at the present time, in relation to that position and corresponding traits sought

(1=Unskilled; 2=Minimum; 3=Adequate; 4=Proficient; 5=No Improvement Needed).

As a leader, this template will allow you to facilitate more effective dialogue and stimulate a thorough conversational interview with the candidates you meet. You will want to have all interviewers use this same template when meeting with candidates. When finished with the interviewing process, collect all profile instrument pages and cross-reference how others scored the candidates' "Skill Level Possession" side of the score sheets.

Some of the variables that may need to be added to the CENTER of the page, where the **"Trait Competency/ Behavior/Skill"** category appears, could be:

1. Basic functionality needs for a position and the obvious corresponding traits necessary to execute that need, which the immediate supervisor desires, that may not come to the surface from the above due diligence.

2. Coworker complementing needs to add to the overall functionality of the team.

3. Immediate management needs, from a position that may not come to the surface from the above due diligence.

4. Immediate and future needs and expectations from the organization of a position should also be added.

To further enhance the effectiveness of the assessment instrument you develop and use, another section for assessment should be **"Position Auditions"**.

Evaluating candidates for your team and determining their true net worth is compounded by governmental legislation, which precludes one from asking many of the core questions needed. This is due, in large part, to the election of mediocre individuals to Congress and its subsequent cascade of legislation and EEOC regulations that protect poor performers and cause the passing of one organization's baggage to others. Witness the trauma in the media today of priests, teachers and employees at large, who, when significant crises arise, the media then learns that their behavior has been systemic and historic in nature.

A means of determining how one may enrich a team is to create a real-to-life scenario audition for each candidate. Just as an actor reveals information via answers to questions and his or her resume in an interview for a part in a motion picture, it is the actual audition of that actor that affords the director (equivalent to the business managerial-leader) a glimpse into the raw talent that they potentially bring to the role if hired.

Some businesses accomplish this by providing a candidate a paid tenure (one or two day) exposure into a position as a ride-along with a sales professional in the field or working at the customer contact window in a retail outlet, etc.

This **"Personal Performance Interview Assessment Instrument"** and accompanying "Position Audition" will provide valuable information in determining who should be added to your winning teams and how you can meet your future needs head-on with confidence as a Legendary Leader!

The following is a template to be used as your **Personal Performance Interview Assessment Instrument©.**

Personnel Performance Survey
Competency/Performance/Behavior/Skill Level Index©
©JEFF MAGEE INTERNATIONAL/JMI, Inc.

Scale

Importance	Skill Level
1 = Not required	1 = Unskilled
2 = Nice to have	2 = Minimum
3 = Basic requirement	3 = Adequate
4 = Important	4 = Proficient
5 = Key	5 = No Improvement Needed

IMPORTANCE   **SKILL LEVEL**

5 4 3 2 1 _____ 1 2 3 4 5
5 4 3 2 1 _____ 1 2 3 4 5
5 4 3 2 1 _____ 1 2 3 4 5
5 4 3 2 1 _____ 1 2 3 4 5
5 4 3 2 1 _____ 1 2 3 4 5
5 4 3 2 1 _____ 1 2 3 4 5
5 4 3 2 1 _____ 1 2 3 4 5
5 4 3 2 1 _____ 1 2 3 4 5
5 4 3 2 1 _____ 1 2 3 4 5
5 4 3 2 1 _____ 1 2 3 4 5
5 4 3 2 1 _____ 1 2 3 4 5
5 4 3 2 1 _____ 1 2 3 4 5
5 4 3 2 1 _____ 1 2 3 4 5
5 4 3 2 1 _____ 1 2 3 4 5
5 4 3 2 1 _____ 1 2 3 4 5
5 4 3 2 1 _____ 1 2 3 4 5
5 4 3 2 1 _____ 1 2 3 4 5
5 4 3 2 1 _____ 1 2 3 4 5

Chapter FIFTY-ONE
Assessment to Success:
What Gets Measured, Gets Measured

"Leading The Way Back, The Leader (mentality)
As The CEO's (mentality) Role..."
- Chief Executive Magazine, November 2002

As a legendary leader, taking stock of your stock can mean the difference between surviving and establishing the benchmark by which others measure performance, productivity, and profitability.

As a managerial-leader today, your ability to continually engage in the development of the key influence leaders in your inner circle and make it so transparent that this assessment ability cascades to all levels within an organization will be an essential art and skill of today's emerging managerial-leader and tomorrow's legendary leader.

Given the limitations in how an organization can interview, assess or terminate non-essential people, combined with the overwhelming regulations and laws that limit effective engagement of these personnel assets. Most organizations have actually given up on truly developing their most powerful asset – their people!

A powerful means for enhancing interview effectiveness and employee assessment, while objectively holding performance accountable is the active and regular use of a Position/Player/Employee Assessment instrument *(if you*

*don't have an effective instrument, either go to
www.JeffreyMagee.com/library.asp and order YIELD
MANAGEMENT for a complete section on designing a
productive and success-oriented instrument or replicate the
model presented.).*

Most organizations have an employee assessment
instrument, which they refer to once or twice annually. The
reality of using such an instrument in that manner serves
only as a legal or human resource protection device.

An effective leader realizes that, even if an organization
stipulates a one or two time a year use approach, they must
use them informally every month. The only way to improve
performance, catch poor habits in the making and coach
performance to peak levels of effectiveness is to measure
objectively and thoroughly on a regular basis.

*What gets measured by managerial-leaders
is what gets measured for improvement!*

Consider using an Assessment Instrument in the following
ways:

1. ***Use The Instrument Globally:*** Use an assessment
   that identifies from minimum to ideal performance
   expectations, as indexed against known predetermined variables required, such as: skill,
   experience, and ability levels necessary for
   performance and production for each core
   functional position on your present team. Including
   yourself, assess every member of you team, peers
   and competition for benchmark information
   monthly, if not even more routinely. No one is
   exempt from this process!

2. *Use the Instrument as a 360:* Use an assessment instrument for true performance improvement purpose by having all directly interacting individuals assess one another (horizontally and vertically-placed personnel). The intention of the assessment instrument is to measure, score, and determine performance development. Any areas for improvement should be noted, and specific action-oriented improvement plans also need to be provided. By exempting no one from the process, everyone will recognize that continuous performance improvement is the constant goal; everyone holds everyone accountable to organizational success!

3. *Use the Instrument to Drive Leadership Development Questions:* Use an assessment personally to drive three hard questions. FIRST, what have you done since the last assessment to develop your skill, knowledge, formal-informal education base, and interpersonal capabilities? SECOND, what do you need to be doing to address immediate needs in respect to skill, knowledge, formal-informal education base acquisition, or interpersonal skills? THIRD, what must you commit to, as the model of leadership excellence, in respect to skill, knowledge, formal-informal education base attainment, or interpersonal skills in the future to meet both your leadership role expectations and those of the evolving organization?

4. ***Use the Instrument for Interviewing and Promoting:*** Once designed, use an assessment instrument for a targeted position to facilitate thorough interviews for new candidates, new positions, existing positions, promotions, and succession planning purposes.

   If energy has been invested into producing an assessment for legal and human resource tracking purposes, ensure that the instrument details both the "tasks" a position is responsible for and the corresponding "traits" an individual should possess to facilitate that "task." Then, use that same instrument to drive the advertising of position openings and facilitation of thorough interviews. In an interview, provide a copy to the candidate and go through each measurement item. Dialogue each measurement item with the other person ... listen for actual responses and for non-verbal responses in determining the candidate's viability.

5. ***Use the Instrument for Alignment:*** Use an assessment instrument to determine if, in fact, you have the right people in the right positions. The assessment of tasks, jobs, projects, committees, etc. will reveal where individuals may presently be assigned or dispatched and, thus, opportunities to adjust players and assigned work-flow for greater efficiencies!

6. ***Design Functionality and Utility:*** The instrument should be easy and fair to administer. Consider three simple scores or assessment qualifiers for each category to be measured – (ONE) *Does Not Meet Expectations – (TWO) Meets Expectations –*

(THREE) Exceeds Expectations. Be aggressive in your assessments. For example, if an individual performs as expected when they were hired, the best score in a given category they can ever attain would be *Meets Expectations.* Conversely, merely going beyond expectations does not earn an *Exceeds Expectations* score; this score is objectively and fairly noted when a person regularly surpasses the expectations of their position and their peer group! Someone can be a good person, but if they do not fulfill the expectations in a scored or measured category, *Does Not Meet Expectations* must be noted for that measurement period!

Create assessment categories for your instrument Then underneath each category header, you can add or delete actual measurement functions, traits, performances, behaviors, actions, interpersonal acts, etc...and they can be modified across organizational lines for positions.

As a leader, using an assessment instrument across all functioning business lines, encompassing all exempt and non-expect personnel, and executed on a regular consistent basis will lead to an ability to continually determine what gets measured, and what gets measured, gets addressed for success!

A leader is about continually developing the players around them. This investment into the personnel assets of the team is a strategic action today that ensures greater tactical effectiveness within the organization for everyone tomorrow.

CONCLUSION –
SECTION SIXTEEN:
Building a Legendary Leader

Chapter 52   Building A Legendary Leader:
The Evolving and Continuing
Process

Chapter FIFTY-TWO
Building a Legendary Leader: To Build a Leader, One Must Embrace an Evolving and Continuing Process That Starts Within the Leader's Mirror

"Good management-leadership consists of showing average people how to do the work of superior people."
- John D. Rockefeller, Jr.

Crafting leadership greatness takes conscious effort, persistent core behaviors, and dedication. When one encounters such a person, the energy forces that erupt from that exposure are those of which legacies are made.

The architecture of *"Building a Legendary Leadership Persona"* can be crafted, honed, and replicated only when one has discovered the unwavering ingredients. Research cited within my weekly syndicated leadership column for the past few years, studies from luminaries past, present, and on-going, as well as exposure to businesses today that many would benchmark as the leaders in productivity and profitability reveals the indisputable activities, programs, and formal and informal efforts continually revolve around fifteen synergy centers.

True legendary leaders realize the need and, thus, demonstrate a commitment to sixteen key factors:

1. Mentoring Future Leaders
2. Developing Thought-Leader Capacity
3. Motivating The Individual
4. Building Political Capital
5. Cultivating and Harvesting Independent Thought Capacity
6. Centering and Balancing
7. Conflict Management and Resolution Abilities
8. Life Balance For Sustained Growth
9. Leadership Engagement Effectiveness
10. Generational Connectedness
11. Controlled Risk-Taking Abilities
12. Leadership Ethics
13. Building A Loyalty Advantage
14. Dealing With The Entitlement Mentality
15. Assessing What Matters, and Continuously Building Upon That Finding
16. Pulling Together The Legendary Leader Behaviors, Beliefs, and Persona

Long before Tom Peters went public in 2002 and owned up to fabricating much of what was written in, *IN SEARCH OF EXCELLENCE*, many business practitioners and certified management consultants were noting that his citations and models did not add up; I was among that body.

As recently detailed in *FROM GOOD TO GREAT*, the perimeters from which one measures a truly legendary leader or organization should be from sustained benchmarks.

Among the leading market business forces today, where this can vividly been seen, are the medical, health care, and pharmaceutical organizations. More specifically, within the pharmaceutical industry, there are examples of legendary leaders and institutions. Some thrive and some merely last another day to survive.

For the past seven consecutive years, doctors and hospital administrators have rated Pfizer Pharmaceutical as the number one organization of choice to deal and work with, as reported in ***Pharmaceutical REPRESENTATIVE magazine.***

In working intimately with Pfizer Pharmaceutical and many other industry notables within the pharmaceutical and biotech industry over the past decade, from the executive team to the front line leadership field team, these sixteen hallmarks have been actively noted.

And, amazingly personally noticed with every business we studied or worked with while in their ascent or at their peak, each consciously or unconsciously subscribed to these synergy points. (doesn't make sense) Each can also directly trace their demise back to the relinquishing of each!

"Success is in the journey and not the destination,"™ and with true leadership effectiveness, leaders have learned to focus upon the ability of asking powerful questions to uncover powerful solutions to compelling needs. The questions reveal the answers, and greatness comes from that journey.

In "Building a Legendary Leader," how do you go about your internal and external processes of building a leader? Are you the one that embraces an evolving and continuing process that starts with what you see in the mirror?

A LEGENDARY LEADER'S legacy is that which can be measured after they are gone from the presence of others and the organization of which they had stewardship!

Dr. Jeffrey L. Magee, PDM, CSP, CMC is a highly sought content rich platform speaker, author, consultant and syndicated leadership columnist. Jeff works with individuals and businesses that wish to greatly increase their productivity and profitability through business and leadership training without limits. He can be reached at Jeff@JeffreyMagee.com, toll free 1-877-90-MAGEE or www.JeffreyMagee.com.

His client's include the leading Fortune 100 firms, major Associations and the largest leadership development organizations in the World. The Department Of Defense commissioned three of Jeff's leadership programs for training their senior officers, senior non commissioned officers and an advanced recruiter selling course nationally to the United States ARMY National Guards 5,000 plus recruiters.

For More Information On Scheduling Magee For Your Next Program Needs, Contact: Robert@JeffreyMagee.com

For Additional Self Development Products:
www.JeffreyMagee.com/library.asp
www.KeepingTheEdge.com

To Enroll Into A Weekly Leadership eZine Newsletter:
http://www.jeffreymagee.com/Newsletter.asp

Jeffrey Magee, Ph.D., PDM, CSP, CMC c/o:
JEFF MAGEE INTERNATIONAL/JMI, Inc.
P. O. Box 701918, Tulsa, OK, 74170-1918
Toll free 1-877-90-MAGEE
www.JeffreyMagee.com

Wallet Reminder Card:
This wallet reminder card can be folded and torn/cut out from this page and carried in your day planner, portfolio, laminated and left on your desk as a quick reference guide to ensure you are always building a legacy and not tearing one down...

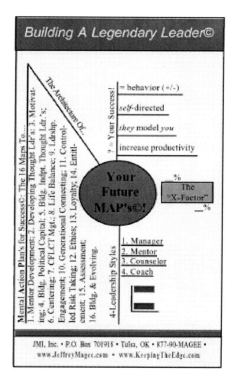